BACK THIS WAY

Memoirs of a Despatch Rider Volume 2

S. P. Muir

Back This Way Copyright © 2020 by S. P. Muir. All Rights Reserved.

All rights reserved. No part of this book may be reproduced in any form or by any electronic or mechanical means including information storage and retrieval systems, without permission in writing from the author. The only exception is by a reviewer, who may quote short excerpts in a review.

Cover designed by S. P. Muir

Visit my website at www.spmuir.com

ISBN- 9798636822028

To all you bikers, old and young. Ride safe, brothers, but ride hard.

BOOKS BY S. P. MUIR
Motorcycle Books:

1) You're Where Now? - Memoirs of a Despatch Rider

2) Back This Way - Memoirs of a Despatch Rider Volume 2

3) Call Me Empty   Memoirs of a Despatch rider volume 3

Fantasy Books:
The saga of the Twins of Arl

1 – The Talisman of Wrath

2 – A War of Destiny

3 – Kamarill: The Earthsoul

INTRODUCTION

I began the first book in this series with the words, "I've been asked many times to write this book." And that of course was true. Well I have to say that I'm absolutely delighted with – and to be honest, rather surprised by – the reaction to *'You're Where Now?'* I'm also extremely grateful for the positive reviews it has received. I was also surprised by the number of people who asked for – nay, demanded – a second volume. How could I refuse?

So, dear reader, here it is: the second collection of anecdotes, memories, and hopefully, some informative words of 'wisdom'. I must stress however, that although this is indeed the second book, I don't believe it's necessary to have read the first book before this one. As I write, it's my intention that it could be a 'stand-alone' volume.

There should be no need to read the two in order – although it probably would be beneficial to do so.

There is one little detail I need to clear up though. An awful lot of people have said something along the lines of, "You idiot Muir; it's spelt *dis*patch, not *des*patch!" In a way they're right; it usually is spelt with an 'i' but despatch with an 'e' is a rarely used but accepted alternative spelling. You might be wondering why I use the alternative spelling if it is so rarely used. The answer is simple. Almost no despatch companies actually called themselves despatch companies on their logos. However, I once rode for a company called, 'Security Despatch' and that spelling sort of stuck in my head.

Now that one's cleared up I feel I should explain the title of the book. The title of the first offering, *'You're where now?'* obviously referred to the question the controller would ask to ascertain the rider's location. This usually was a good thing because it meant he had another pickup for you; which in turn meant more money. 'Back this way' usually meant disappointment though. As soon as you'd delivered all your packages you'd call (or phone) in 'empty'. If it was getting late and you were near home, you'd hope to hear, "slide off home from there." So to hear, "Back this way" was a real blow.

At any other time you wanted to hear that he had another job to take you back to town. No dead mileage, hooray! Most of the time, however, he would just say those hated words, "Back this way."

Title apart, this book is pretty much the same as the first except for chapter 11, 'Workhorses'. Here I wax lyrical about some of the bikes we used. In reality, these were the unsung heroes of the motorcycle courier business. The reason I felt the need to pen this particular section is simple: once again I was asked to do so. I know my father's eyes (along with those of quite a few other readers) will glaze over and they'll probably skip that chapter altogether. If that's the case let me apologise in advance. But the truth is, most readers will be bikers themselves. As such, I hope they'll be interested and perhaps even surprised by some of my comments about those sturdy (and not so sturdy) workhorses of old.

On a different subject, there is something else I need to address. I've given the impression that we all used to hurtle around the streets of London with our throttles wide open while giving scant regard to our own or anyone else's safety. This wasn't actually the case. True, we used to move pretty quickly – which to those watching looked rather scary – but the way to knock out as many deliveries as possible had more to do with knowing your way around than crying 'Banzai' and throwing all caution to the wind. Those that did didn't last very long. One rider I knew rode very sedately indeed, and yet he was always one of the top earners. His forensic knowledge of London's backstreet shortcuts more than made up for his gentle riding style. He really was one of the best of the best.

As before, I've taken the liberty of changing some names and locations. This is to protect the innocent – and not so innocent – from any repercussions that might ensue. The names of my close friends, however, remain unchanged.

But that's enough preamble, let's get on with it. Let us once again step through the mirror into the wonderland of eighties London. Breathe in the diesel fumes and listen to the roar of the bikes; hear the angry cries of, "Oi, you've broken my effing wing mirror!" I hope you all like it as much as you appear to have enjoyed *'You're Where Now?'*

1: FILLER CAP BLUES

Every now and then in the despatch industry there would be an earlier than usual collection booked for the next morning. A bike would often then be assigned that collection the night before – something that was always one of the more sought after jobs. Occasionally, you'd also pick up the package the night before, ready to deliver it when the recipient opened their doors first thing in the morning. At the smaller courier companies these little pearls would often be handed out in the office at the end of the day. And if it was a particularly nice job – a plum, as they were often known – it would frequently be doled out very quietly. Perhaps the rider concerned would be the controller's favourite (they weren't supposed to have favourites but they usually did) or it was in return for that rider doing the controller a favour.

For whatever the reason, keeping such things quiet was usually a good policy.

There were many benefits to working for a small outfit, the close camaraderie being one of them. But that same tightknit relationship could also lead to jealousy and bitterness – especially if it was felt that just one rider was getting all the sweeties in the jar. Larger companies were different in as much as the riders seldom went to the office. Some only saw the place on payday or if their radio went on the fritz. The plum jobs, therefore, usually went out over the air. Although there were ways around it, the greater transparency did allow a far more equitable distribution of wealth.

I was working for one of the smaller outfits at the time of this particular anecdote. I'd quietly been given an early morning start at last knockings the night before. I'd collected the package and taken it home ready to be delivered at eight-thirty the next morning. The client just happened to be one of our top accounts in the west end.

The delivery was in slough which paid a decent twelve quid at the time. This meant that even if I did have the dreaded "Back this way," I'd be back 'in the middle' by nine-thirty at the latest. I'd be there just as the work was really beginning to come in – and with almost a quarter of my day's money in the bag to boot!

It was winter and the weather was cold and icy. The gritter lorries had been kept pretty busy and that meant a lot of salt on the road which ended up all over the bike. This was something I always tried to keep on top of since it could corrode your engine casings, damage your chain, and even play tricks with your electrics. But this time there was one thing I wasn't prepared for.

I was a happy little bunny as I made my way home that evening. I cut my way through the rush hour traffic jam with the package in my top box and a definite spring in my step, so to speak. As I went, I ran through the things I needed to do to be ready for my early start. Normally I did my bike checks in the morning but just to be sure, I decided to do them all that night.

"Tum tee tum, fill up with petrol; da dee da, tighten and oil the chain; doo dee doo; tyre pressures; la lee la, check the oil." It was the first on the list that caused me the problem.

As usual, I pulled into my local petrol station to fill up. I jumped gleefully off the bike and took my gloves off. I laid them on the engine to warm up which was a trick all hardened bikers quickly learn. I put the key in the filler cap lock and tried to turn it. Nothing. It was jammed fast. I wiggled it, I jiggled it, I tapped it, and I thumped it. Nothing. Even swearing at it made no difference; it just wasn't going to budge. The road salt had well and truly worked its way in and had corroded the innards. There was nothing for it but to carry on home and fix it there.

Less than five minutes later I arrived at my house. I was cold and hungry but dinner would just have to wait; I was a man on a mission. The remedy was obvious and simple: WD40. This marvellous spray is the cure-all for just this sort of problem. It penetrates, lubricates, and dispels water. It's a must for all bikers and I had plenty of it to hand. What I didn't have was a garage, a shed, or even an outside light. But no matter, I had the torch which I'd been planning to use to do my checks; and how much light do you need to squirt a lock? Double-Yew-Dee even has a straw that just about fits into the keyhole. Just a quick squirt into the lock, a bit of wiggling with the key, and hey presto, the cap'll be off.

I got my torch out but to my dismay, it didn't work. The damn battery was flat. I let out a quiet but extremely frustrated expletive. I took a deep breath and forced myself to stay calm. After all, I repeated, how much light does it take to poke the little straw into the keyhole? True enough, I successfully managed to poke it in. I gave it a quick squirt, then put the key in and wiggled it. Hey presto... nothing. It was absolutely jammed solid. There was only one thing to do.

"I'm bringing the bike indoors," I said to the wife.

"You're bloody not," she replied angrily – a response I could quite understand since the only room I could get the bike into was the lounge. And since we had a lovely and rather expensive carpet in that room...

"I bloody am!" I retorted firmly. "I've got to sort it out for the morning."

"You'll just have to sort it *in* the morning. Do it before you go in. That's what you normally do; if you're late you're late."

Patiently, I went on to explain why it had to be mended that night. Patiently she listened, and with great understanding said, "You're still not bringing it in!"

Thankfully, one of her friends, Fran, was there which helped to prevent a full-blown row erupting. But even so there was a loud and angry standoff. Eventually it was agreed that if I first put half a rain forest of newspaper on the floor, I *could* bring it in for the repair. With a somewhat frosty "thank you," I went and got the bike.

The machine in question was a bright red Suzuki GSX400EZ. Not the biggest bike in the world but still a proper faff to wriggle through the front door without damaging the woodwork. So a full hour after pulling up at my house, I got to work on the recalcitrant filler cap in earnest.

"Hmm..." I said thoughtfully as I peered into the lock's innards. "I can't see why it won't..." I'd squirted a good half a can of WD40 into it to no avail, so what on earth was the problem? I decided to give 'Three-in-One' oil a try. It doesn't penetrate as effectively but it does do a better job of lubricating. Still nothing. I decided to clean myself up, have some dinner, and then give it another go. Perhaps once it had warmed up in the lounge it might be more co-operative.

I finished eating, drank my coffee, and smoked another cigarette, all the while thinking what a good ornament the bike made. I then attacked the problem with a little more patience and calm. It didn't last.

"F***ing thing!" I screamed "What am I going to do?"

"Can't you just do the job and then sort it out after?" Fran asked. It was a reasonable enough question but I was no longer in a reasonable mood. "No I bloody can't," I snapped. "I haven't got enough petrol left in the bloody tank!"

"Oh, I see," she said quietly. The poor woman looked more than a little taken aback by my ire, but I was far too stressed to care. She quickly made her excuses and left.

"Now see what you've done!" the missus barked furiously. But even her fiery, often explosive temperament balked under the withering fury of the look I gave her. She very shrewdly left me to it.

In the end there was only one answer: there was nothing for it but sheer brute force! Okay, when I was finished any type of key would fit the mangled lock, but let's face it, how often does someone nefariously try to open a filler cap? Exactly! I proceeded with gusto. To achieve the required end I needed the right screwdriver – one that was small enough to fit into the keyhole but meaty enough to take the strain. I was lucky enough to have one just the right size. I also possessed a good sized hammer and some large mole-grips.

I hammered the screwdriver into the lock and then clamped the mole-grips onto the handle.

I've had to resort to forcing locks before so I knew roughly how much pressure to apply. Nothing. "What the...?" With a puzzled frown I applied some more pressure, and then even more. Nothing.

In the end I felt like a dentist trying to extract a particularly difficult wisdom tooth. You've probably seen the picture. The dentist has his plyers gripping the tooth, he has one foot on the poor patient's shoulder and is heaving away for all he's worth with the sweat pouring down his face. Of course, just as that tooth is eventually going to give, so did the lock – in a way.

With a sudden loud '*crack*', the damn thing exploded. I kid you not; tiny bits of metal sprayed across the room like shrapnel. I was dumbfounded. I just couldn't understand what had happened. There was no longer a lock to put a key into.

On the bright side, the cap was off. With the benefit of a small screwdriver I could fill up the tank and do the early morning job. The real downfall was the fact that a new filler cap was going to cost more than the twelve quid the job paid; that and the howls of derisive laughter coming from across the room of course.

2: SPARK UP A FAG AND WAIT

Breakdowns were at best a pain in the backside, but they could also be one of your worst nightmares come to life. As I described in the last chapter, even something as simple as a jammed lock could be the cause of panic and imminent disaster – and that was in the comfort of my own home! Some breakdowns could be fixed at the side of the road and I prided myself on my ability to 'bodge' a usable roadside repair. I once 'fixed' an MZ Supa 5's gearbox problem with a couple of elastic bands. Crazy, but it got me home.

But the fear of being left high and dry in the middle of nowhere on a dark and stormy night was always with me. Even thirty-odd years later, I sometimes wake up in a cold sweat having suffered that particular nasty dream. A puncture, however, was usually no more than an irritation;

a source of frustration that if you were prepared (see chapter 9) was easily overcome. Not so on one particular winter's evening.

Once again I'm talking about that same GSX400 that suffered the filler cap catastrophe. It was a great bike, and one that I did more miles on than any other bolide that I've abused. And it was quick – really quick. Talk to any biker and he'll tell you that his particular bike is faster than all the other bikes of the same model. I'm sure we all know someone whose bog-standard fizzy did seventy-odd miles an hour!

That aside, my GSX really was the quickest one around. And there was a very good reason for that: it had been run in for no less than ten thousand miles! Not by me of course. Although I was always meticulously gentle with a new bike, even I felt that twelve *hundred* miles was enough.

This bike had been owned by a friend of a friend who was renowned for riding extremely carefully. He was one of those rare bikers who believed that speed limits were carved in stone. I doubt it had ever been above seventy mph in any of those initial ten thousand miles of daily commuting. After about eighteen months he part exchanged it at a dealer near Brands Hatch. As my trusty Honda 400 four was by now pushing seventy thousand miles, I was looking for a new bike. Obviously it had to be a good one, but I could only afford second-hand. When I heard that he'd sold it, I was delirious with anticipation. First thing next morning, I phoned the dealer.

"Yeah, it's still here," they said.

"Great," I exclaimed rather too eagerly. "The thing is I'm looking to PX my Honda 400; would you be interested?" I had every finger crossed and probably a few toes as well. If they said no all bets were off.

"No problem, there's a fair demand for 'em so we'll definitely take it off your hands."

Now came the killer question. "How much will you give me for it?"

I could have heard the sharp intake of breath even without the phone. "I can't really say without seeing it."

"Ah, I see. The problem is it's a very long way for me to come; and if the price isn't right I can't afford the bike."

"Hmm... that is a bit of a problem. How much do need?"

"Three hundred and fifty," I lied. To be honest, I was really pushing my luck. It was the high end even for a pristine seven-year-old, let alone a well-used and frankly abused example. And let's face it, the Suzuki was only up for £795.

Again the sharp intake of breath. "That's a bit steep. What's the mileage; what sort of nick's it in?"

Here it was; the crunch point. There was no point in lying, I had to describe the poor thing accurately – wart's an' all.

"Ooh, sorry; no can do. Hang on a minute though, let me see what's what."

After the longest couple of minutes of my life he came back on the line. "Right, here's the bottom line; the best I can offer you is two-two-five – and that's well above what it's worth."

"Oh dear," I said, trying to sound disappointed. Inside I was turning cartwheels. I didn't think I'd get any more than a hundred and fifty. Oh well, I suppose that'll have to do. I'll be there in a couple of hours. I'll want to take it straight away."

"Erm... right. It's rather short notice but if we prep it for you now... as long as you're definitely coming that is."

"Oh don't worry, I'm coming all right."

So that was that; I went, I saw, I bought. Veni vidi vici. At first its performance was far from blistering –very far! But nonetheless it was a really nice ride. And anyway, its lacklustre acceleration and disappointing top-end was immaterial; it was its reliability that was important; and with this bike's gentle early years, it was going to be rock solid. As the miles slid by, however, it became clear what the problem was: the engine was still tight! And once it had loosened up, it became a front-wheel-in-the-air pocket rocket.

And that leads me to the evening in question. Work was over and I was hurrying home. For some reason the rush hour traffic was unusually light and I was really hustling. I overtook a sensibly-riding guy on a GPZ550 Kawasaki (the quickest 550 at the time) and continued on my way. I soon became aware that the bloke was up for the challenge, so how could I resist?

He was clearly more than just a commuter, for he was good – very good in fact. It was a real good tussle as we played cat and mouse in and out of the still-plentiful cars. Eventually we pulled up at a set of traffic lights.

"That goes a bit," he said giving my bike an admiring glance.

Beneath my helmet I beamed with pride. "Yeah, it's not bad."

My adversary then fixed his attention on the lights and blipped his throttle meaningfully. The drag race was on.

A fraction of a fraction of a split second after the amber appeared, we screamed away from the line. I threw my weight forward to keep the front end down and miracle of miracles, my humble 400 was half a bike length in front. The latest, fastest, meanest, superdooperest (that is now officially a word) middleweight on the market was getting a drubbing. A few seconds later we caught up with the traffic and in an act of pure self-preservation, he allowed me to keep the lead.

It couldn't last, of course. A few minutes later we were on the motorway. I nailed the game little 400's throttle against the stop and stuck my nose between the clocks. It was a futile exercise. The GPZ just walked away, especially when we hit a slight incline. But even then The GSX held 108 mph. Still, what with the laws of physics being so annoyingly predictable, by the time we were on the flat, the GPZ's tail light was but a twinkling red spot in the distance. Even so, I refused to admit defeat. The speedo needle crept inexorably up, as did the rev counter. At 115 it hit the redline, and even then it continued to climb. I must have had a bit of a tailwind – either that or my bike was as stubborn as I was. And that was when it happened – a blowout.

Now I've had several sudden deflations before (although none at such a high speed) and I'm well versed in the procedure. Some of it is counter-intuitive and not so well known in this age of high performance tubeless tyres. Back then, most tyres had inner tubes. At the risk of teaching my grandmother to suck eggs, I'll quickly run through the technique.

DON'T slam on the brakes! Yes you need to scrub speed off quickly, but hit the brakes and your back wheel will just slide out or even try to overtake your front.

KEEP THE BIKE STRAIGHT. Not always possible, but any attempt at cornering will more than likely spit you off.

And just as important, RELAX. Let the bike shimmy and squirm beneath you. If you tense up or try to fight it, you'll only cause yourself grief.

All of this, however, is the cure for a *back wheel* blowout. The only recourse for a front wheel blowout at speed is... prayer! And boy did I need to pray. The handlebars were throwing themselves from lock to lock so fast it felt like my shoulders were about to be dislocated. If I'd tried to hold them straight I swear the grips would have been torn from my hands. I just let my arms go limp and rode it out.

On this particular stretch of road there was no hard shoulder as such, just a gravelled soft verge – a providential, ready-made gravel trap. My speed was coming down pretty quickly and as it did, the frantically oscillating handlebars eased their demonic attempt to wrest themselves away from me. I was soon able to use the clutch and come down through the gears, carefully utilising just the right amount of engine braking.

Somehow I guided the poor stricken beastie onto the gravel and I was saved.

Actually, I was stranded. Remember, mobile (cell) phones were still around ten years into the future. Apart from the lights of the now rather fewer cars flashing past, it was as black as the earl of hell's waistcoat. My own headlight lit up the road ahead, mocking my inability to travel any further. It did little to illuminate my front wheel, however. But did I panic, did I despair? Of course I didn't!

You see, I'd read Ted Simon's incredible book, *'Jupiter's Travels'*. This intrepid free-lance journalist had once embarked on a round the world ride on a Triumph 500 Speed Twin! Not one of your modern day, purpose built, big-engined adventure bikes. Oh no, a British-made road bike that was already twenty years out of date when it was built. This man had plums the size of cannonballs! And he had Zen. Buy it, read it, and be amazed. I'll repeat the title: *Jupiter's Travels* by Ted Simon.

The most useful pearl of wisdom I gleaned from his book was simply this: when you break down, take a deep breath and relax; sit down beside your bike, spark up a fag and wait. Before you've finished your ciggie help will arrive – no matter where you are. It sounds like real hippie, new-age nonsense, doesn't it? Yet Ted Simon was in the middle of the Sahara and it worked! So surely the side of a motorway was child's play.

True enough, before I was halfway through my first Marlborough, a bread lorry pulled over onto the verge.

"You got a problem?" the driver asked as he jumped down from his cab.

"Yeah; a blowout."

"Where ya goin'"

I told him where I lived.

"That's handy; it's only about a mile out of my way. The back's empty so we can load your bike in and I'll run you home. You'll have to stay in the back with the bike though. You'll need to hold it steady."

I had no problem with that; and even loading the bike on was easy. The van – actually a 7.5 ton lorry – had a hydraulic lift. About twenty minutes later I was home. I only wish I'd had some money in the house to reward my hero of the hour, but all I could offer him was a cup of tea.

But now I can thank him in the pages of this book. Whoever you are and wherever you are, my sincerest thanks go out to you – oh, and also to Ted Simon, obviously.

3: NORWICH

One of the most surreal events I experienced was on one of those incredibly sought-after distance jobs. Great Portland Street going all the way to Norwich. One hundred and twenty warm and sunny, summer miles. And of course, being summer the circuit was dead.

It was late in the morning and all I'd done was three local deliveries. I hadn't even made a tenner, and the way things were going, I'd be extremely lucky to make twenty quid by the end of the day. But here was a plum job worth about fifty-five of our lovely British pound notes.

I rushed round to the pickup and was soon standing beside the bike – a Honda 400 four – with the small package safely tucked away in my top box. I lit up a ciggie and drew in a huge lungful of delicious JPS smoke. It would I knew, be my last chance for a puff for a couple of hours.

"Three-three," I chirruped happily into the quiescent radio.

"Three-three," came the immediate reply. This was one of the few benefits of a quiet circuit; you didn't have to fight to get heard above all the other riders.

"Three-three, pee-oh-bee going Norwich." I was crossing my fingers hoping for another job going the same way. A few extra quid would be a real cherry on the top. When it's busy you could almost guarantee another drop on the way, but on a really slack day like today?

"Carry on, three-three; phone me empty."

"Yeah, roger-'odge." There wasn't too much disappointment in my voice. If there really *was* something going in the same direction, it was only fair that some other poor desperate sod got the benefit. I pulled out my map book and checked the route. A quick wriggle through to Clerkenwell Road and then on to Old Street. Through Hackney, pick up the A12 to Redbridge, and then onto the M11. Follow that for a while and then it was the A11 all the way to Norwich. Easy peasy.

There was one fly in the ointment, however, and that would come when I reached the destination city. You couldn't carry a street map of every town and city in the country; and satnavs existed only in science fiction back then. The idea that a little box could not only tell you where to go but would even give you a choice of routes to take was farcical. You'd have more luck believing in some kind of magic – a sixth sense that could at least guide you to the side of town you needed! Like most long-term despatch riders, I had just that magical ability – or so it seemed, anyway. I put everything away, stamped out my fag, and pulled on my crash hat. I was off.

The traffic was light as I threaded my way through the centre of town, and there was no need to rush. There was no deadline for the package, it just needed to get there sometime in the afternoon. In spite of my leisurely pace, I was soon out onto the M11. I wound the little four up to a sedate, fuel-sipping sixty-five and settled myself into the saddle. It was glorious. The sun was shining, the scenery was pretty, and the cooling air was flowing comfortably around my overheated body. With the Honda's low bars and ergonomically sorted riding position, this was shaping up to be a serene and restful ride.

The bike purred contentedly all the way to Norwich where I followed my nose towards where my gut told me I needed to be. All I had to do now was ask for directions. Pretty soon I spotted someone and I swept up beside him.

It's funny, but I remember the name of the street I wanted as if it's been seared into my mind with a branding Iron. Yet when I looked on google maps today, it wasn't there. Have I remembered it wrong, I wondered? Perhaps I have, but I'm as certain as I can be that I haven't.

"Excuse me," I called as politely as I could from beneath my helmet. "Do you know where Upper Street North is?"

The man looked at me with his oddly bright grey eyes, and then with a line that could have come straight out of a comedy sketch said, "Yeah I know." Then, with a strangely vacant expression on his face, he turned and walked away. His blank mien and determined stride made it clear that the conversation was over.

"Oh well," I thought, "perhaps he's just got a thing against bikers." It was, after all, a common enough prejudice back then and probably still is. So undeterred I carried on.

I'd not gone far when I spied a woman. I duly pulled up beside her and asked for directions. This time, however, I phrased the question more carefully. "Excuse me, could you *tell me* where Upper Street north is?"

Now at this point in my tale, I'm afraid I'm going to have to say something controversial. Among us despatch riders there was an unwritten rule. Today it would be regarded as offensively sexist and even misogynistic; but even the female riders in our ranks agreed with it.

The decree stated that unless absolutely necessary, you should *never* ask a woman for directions. As a rule of thumb – or so it was said – it was a pointless exercise. Not because the female of the species was in any way considered inferior, and they certainly weren't thought of as stupid. Indeed, they were just as likely to know where you needed to go as any man. The problem would always be in the way women related that information. There was just too much of it.

Rather than an easily digested, "Go straight on for about a mile until you pass the BP station, and then it's third on the right." You'd more than likely get: "Go straight on past the church on your left. You can't miss it, it's really big. Keep going on past the park and eventually you'll pass a petrol station. The road you want is third on the right after that. If you come to another church, you've gone too far and you'll have to turn around. Then it'll be, let me see, yes, second on your left."

All an extremely accurate and far more detailed explanation. It would also be more helpful than the man's directions if only we poor stupid men could remember it all. But in fact, it's just TMI – information overload.

Now before all my female readers explode with indignant rage and delete this book or throw it onto a bonfire, let me just add that it wasn't necessarily a rule born out in fact. In my own experience, however, there was more than a grain of truth in it. Even so I needn't have worried on this occasion. Her answer was very brief and succinct.

"Of course I can, my love. It's behind the market." With a lovely warm smile and a friendly twinkle in her vacant and somewhat familiar, bright grey eyes, she turned and walked away.

It took just a second or two for my dumbfounded silence to evaporate, but even that was too long. "But where's the market?" I called after her. It was pointless; she was gone. I muttered a frustrated cuss word, stamped the four hundred into gear and continued my search.

Aha; a smartly dressed man in a suit. Surely I'd get a more sensible response from him. Once again I pulled up alongside and asked an even more carefully phrased question.

"Excuse me, sir, could you *direct me* to Upper Street North? I've been told it's behind the market, but I don't know where the market is."

The man smiled at me and my stomach sank. His eyes were a lovely bright grey that twinkled with vacant friendliness. This was the third time in a matter of minutes that I'd seen those exact same eyes.

"You can't mistake the market; it's near the police station." This time, as the source of my frustration walked away, I didn't even have the strength of will to call out for more information. I just sat there in open mouthed disbelief. I felt as though I'd stepped into an episode of the Twilight Zone. Eventually though, I ventured on my way once again.

Then I saw him. Back then they belonged to the police; a much reviled bird with a distinctive plumage; the *Lesser, Yellow-Striped, Traffic Vulture*. As much as I loathed the creatures, surely this one would be able to give me coherent directions.

"Excuse me," I began warily. "Can you give me directions to Upper Street North? I *know* it's behind the market, and I *know* the market's near the police station, but I need *directions*!"

The traffic warden turned to me and grinned. To my immense relief his eyes weren't bright grey, dark grey, blue-grey, nor any other shade of flaming grey! They were brown! Proper brown. Real non-twilight zone brown. And to be honest, I couldn't have cared less if they were a satanic jet-black.

"Course I can chum," he said with a pure and blessed cockney accent. "Keep going straight on for a bit and you'll pass the police station. When you get to the market, hang a left and follow it round to the back. On your left you'll see a sort of ramp; go up that and you're there."

"You're not from round here, are you," I stated with absolute certainty.

"Nah mate; hackney born and bred."

With my heartfelt thanks ringing in his ears, I shot off following his succinct and accurate directions. In no time at all, my package was delivered safe and sound. Then obediently, I phoned in.

"Hi, it's three three. I'm empty in Norwich."

"Hang on," the telephonist replied. There was a pause and in the background I could hear her muffled voice repeating what I'd said to the controller.

A moment later the controller was on the line. "Well done. Obviously nothing for you up there, so back this way."

It was only about one-forty-five, so I could probably get back to town for around half-past-four. I knew I was taking a liberty but it was dead, so...

"Erm, I thought I might slide off home from here."

"Yeah, go on then; but keep your radio on and give me a call when you get in range. You never know, there might be something to bring you back into town."

"Of course I will," I lied. Sorry, but there was no way I was going back to work now. I'd earned a good day's money and my mind was already at home with my feet up, a ciggie in one hand and a nice cold drink in the other. So after a celebratory cigarette in Norwich, I set off to make that wonderful mental picture a reality.

As I pootled back down the motorway I pondered on the strange, grey-eyed people I'd met. Were they typical of the locals? Was every indigenous inhabitant of Norwich some kind of inbred village idiot, or had I momentarily strayed into some odd, alternate reality populated by strange, grey-eyed fools. At the time I laughed it all off, delighted to have yet another anecdote to regale my friends with. Maybe it was all a coincidence. Perhaps they were all related and were coming away from some kind of family gathering. Yes of course, that *must* be it.

But now that Upper Street North seems never to have existed, I'm not so sure...

4: HOW TO MURDER A FRIEND

The daily commute into town was always a grind. Bumper to bumper office workers and the like, all of them bad tempered and sick of the snarled up, snail's pace they were forced to endure. I have to confess, there were very occasional but extremely delicious feelings of schadenfreude as I swept past some of them. The feelings were usually caused by people in sporty cars; and the schadenfreude would always increase in proportion to the performance of the almost-parked car. It was funny enough when it was an Escort XR3i or a Golf GTi, but the sight of a Ferrari or Lamborghini would have me almost crying with laughter. It didn't matter how much power he had under his bonnet, the Thatcherite, city-slicker yuppie behind the wheel was as stuck as the bloke in the clapped out, fifty-quid Cortina in front of him.

But the tiresome crawl into work wasn't the only source of their frustration. Whatever car the poor commuters had, their patience was also under constant assault from the steady stream of bikes whizzing past their right elbow. It must have been even more annoying when they'd just had their wing mirror clipped for the umpteenth time that month. And when it's been smashed for the third time that year?

Of course, the packed roads were vexing enough even for us bikers, but every now and then the journey could be brightened up. When you came across a rider you'd seen a few times before for instance. And if you saw them regularly enough, you could develop a kind of friendship. Of course, you never spoke, and you'd only recognise them by their bike and their crash helmet, but even so there'd be a kind of bond. If you happened across one of your *real* friends though, the grind could actually become enjoyable. Often, those times would turn into a game as the man in front would try and shake off the man behind; hardly a race but a good game nonetheless. And there's one particular game that has stayed with me all these years.

On that fateful morning, I had one of the several CD200s I've owned, and my friend Gary had... Do you know, I can't remember and neither can he. I do remember that he and my other friend Jez used to buy a bike between them – a CX or its like – and share the commute and the costs together. Their main bikes would thus be spared the travails and high mileages of workaday life. But on this particular morning, Gary was alone and as he had a predilection for big'uns, I have a feeling he was on his lime green, Eddie Lawson replica, Z1100R Kawasaki. Whatever it was though, it wasn't small.

We met up at the end of a fast A road which was never really fast at that time of the day. He politely slotted in behind me and we soon entered the snarled up ordinary road. Obviously my little 200 Benly now had the advantage, and it was one I now began to exploit to the full. As I flew down the outside of the traffic I would every now and then glance in my mirror to see how he was doing. As a regular commuter and a dedicated, all weather, 'use your bike instead of your car' type of man, he was – and probably still is – a better than average rider. Because of that he was easily managing to stay with me. I was not amused. I pushed harder and harder until I was wringing the poor little Benly's neck in an effort to get away.

At this point I need to explain something. It sounds to the uninitiated that the London commute was simply a matter of riding down the offside of a single line of cars. So why would a big and extremely fast 1100 (if that is indeed what it was) have trouble sitting behind a slow little lightweight? The answer lies in two things: traffic islands and oncoming traffic. There would regularly be a need to slip in between the line (sometimes lines) of cars you were filtering past.

The skill of the game lay in planning ahead, watching for openings or potential openings that you could exploit. Pull into one too early and the bike behind will sail past you; but leave it too late and you could find yourself stopped at an island waiting for a convenient gap. If you were really lucky, a kindly driver would to allow you to push in. Of course, while you're there, your mate passes you on the inside, usually with a smug and irritating little wave. If you're stuck there for too long, you'll never catch up with him. Game, set, and match.

So there we were, blatt, brake, dodge, wriggle and weave, both having a literal blast. I'd managed to pull out a fair lead when the road started to curve round to the left. In spite of the bend I could see some traffic coming the other way (remember, there was almost nothing coming *out* of town) and realised I would need to pull in before I met it. I studied the pattern of the slow moving cars and muttered a disappointed curse. There were no gaps anywhere; it was all a bumper to bumper crawl. Then I saw it; not a gap per se, but a potential opening – if I was lucky. The cars a hundred yards ahead had suddenly accelerated from a snail's pace up to a heady, brisk walk. If someone was just a fraction tardy in following suit, I could force my little Honda into the resulting opening.

Gary was by now storming up behind me and had almost caught up when I hit my brakes and stuffed my bike in front of an aggrieved driver. My best of friends was suddenly confronted by an oncoming tide of cars and/or lorries with absolutely nowhere to go! Quite how he got away with it I can't remember; but I certainly do remember the torrent of abuse I got from him the next time he came round my house.

"You bastard!" he cried furiously. "You deliberately sold me a dummy! You could have killed me, you (expletives deleted) bastard!"

I tried to keep a straight face, I really did; but in all honesty, how could I? If he'd been hurt (or even worse, if his bike had been damaged) I'd have been mortified! But to see him safely standing in front of me and venting his spleen? It was too funny. To this day he'll call me some choice names if it comes up.

But once again, I can now say it in the pages of this book. I can truthfully declare for all the world to read (well I can but hope): Gary, I did *not* try to kill you. I did *not* deliberately sell you that dummy; honestly...

5 THE MAN WITH THE MEDALS

There were a lot of people who had a deep rooted antipathy towards the despatch riding fraternity. I've spoken about the police and black cab drivers in *'You're Where Now?'* but the worst of all were bloody security guards. They were worse than all the others simply because they were the ones we came into contact with the most. Not the heroic types who singlehandedly patrol a lonely industrial complex or deliver huge sums of money to banks and shops, you understand. Those men are taking a real risk for a pittance of pay. Oh no, I mean the ones at the front desks of offices – the men with the medals, as we called them.

Almost to a man, they were trumped-up little jobsworth's in love with their own little bit of power. They seemed to take a great deal of pleasure in being as awkward as possible. Most of the time we put up with their sullen obstinacy with little more than a curse muttered between gritted teeth. Sometimes, however, they completely overstepped the mark. There are many tales I could tell to illustrate the point, but for now I'll stick with just the one. Maybe I'll relate some more if ever I pen a third collection of these anecdotes.

When I first embarked on my despatching mistake...I mean career, I could forgo the slight irritation of removing my crash helmet when I made a pickup or delivery. Even when I had a top box mounted radio with phones and mike velcroed inside my lid, I would put up with it. This system needed careful arranging when you put your hat on, however, or it would be agonisingly uncomfortable. If it was really busy and I had a lot of parcels to knock out as quickly as possible, I wanted to leap off my bike, run into the office, get a signature, and run out again. Time was money so I tended to leave my lid firmly on my head. Most riders were the same.

But as time passed and security measures tightened, we were often asked to remove our lids. If it was a nice receptionist, it would be a polite, "Can you remove your helmet please." Happily we would comply, but the security guard was a different kettle of fish altogether.

"Take your hat off," the worst would demand with a haughty sneer. Grudgingly, we would obey the unnecessarily ill-mannered order. If the rider was having a bad day and the man with the medals was particularly offensive though, it could result in an argument. Those occasions, however, were thankfully rare.

But there was one particular office block where it just went too far. And it was something that disturbingly began to catch on in other places too. It was a block with lots of different companies in it, so you'd have to go to the front desk and tell the security men (there were always at least two) where you wanted to go. Fair enough. I'd been there many times before and anyway, by now I'd got into the habit of removing my bash-hat everywhere I went. I walked up to the front desk and informed them of where I was going.

"Third floor," one of the *three* men stated pointlessly.

"Cheers," I replied in a deliberately happy and friendly voice. I knew there was nothing that pissed some of these guys off more than the knowledge that they'd failed to piss *you* off.

"Leave your crash helmet here."

"What!" I cried incredulously. "Why?"

"Because I said so."

"I don't see why I should."

"Well you're not going in if you don't."

I took a deep breath and tried to stay calm. "Look, I've been here loads of times and I've never had to leave it here before."

"So what," one of the other jobsworth's chipped in. "Some of you lot have been putting them on once they're in the lift. And anyway, no one else has complained." He pointed to a couple of helmets on the floor just behind the desk.

Muttering darkly about the idiots who'd willingly surrendered their expensive helmets to these belligerent numbskulls, I reluctantly handed it over and made my delivery.

The news of this abuse of power spread like wildfire and was the centre of a great deal of resentful chatter among us. Still, at the time it was only one block and there was no choice but to obey. Eventually though, a darker piece of news circulated through our ranks.

It concerned one our comrades who'd treated himself to a top of the range Arai – one of the most expensive helmets on the market. Quite why he'd felt the need to buy one was beyond most of us. Back then helmets were often regarded more as a legal requirement than an important bit of head protection. I'd even taken part in more than one MAG rally, protesting about the law making them compulsory. Even so it was universally admired for the expensive piece of artwork it undoubtedly was. One day this profligate young man had cause to visit the offices in question, and duly handed over his helmet. He did his business and then returned to the front desk.

"Here you are," the security guard had said handing him an old and scratched cheap crash helmet.

"That's not mine."

"Yes it is."

"I should know my own crash hat," our rider allegedly retorted.

It turned out that the idiot behind the desk had given the rider's brand new pride and joy away to someone else. The thieving bit of scum had clearly taken the opportunity to trade up!

Obviously he wouldn't be able to wear it at work because he'd have quickly found himself facing summary justice! But he could flog it to someone else, or even keep it for weekend rides.

The point is, the next time I went to that building I was determined.

"Leave your helmet…"

"No!" I interrupted firmly. "I'll take it with me thank you."

"You're not going in if…"

I'd already prepared my response so I interrupted him again. "No problem. I will leave it here, but only if you give me a written guarantee that you'll replace it if you lose it – or give it away to someone else," I added with a malicious smirk.

"You're not getting that."

"Then you're not getting my helmet."

"Then you're not getting in."

"Fine," I said playing my trump card. "Then you'd better phone up and tell Mrs Smith (not her real name) that she won't be getting her *very* urgent package."

"I'll be damned if I will!"

"Fine," I said again with a pugnacious grin. I hit the key on my radio. "Three-three."

"Tree-three," came the fortuitously swift reply.

"Yeah, three-three, I'm at the drop-off but the man with the medals won't let me in without surrendering my lid." The guard bristled indignantly at his disparaging new epithet.

"Can't you just... oh gawd, you're *there*, aren't you." The tale of the missing Arai had obviously percolated up to the controllers.

"Roger."

"Can't you leave the package at the desk?"

"No can do. I was told to hand it to her personally. It's really important, apparently."

"Roger, three-three; wait there. I'm on the phone gents," he added, letting everyone else know not to call in for a while.

A couple of minutes passed during which, if looks could kill I'd have crumbled to dust.

"Three-three," my radio eventually squawked.

"Yeah, three-three."

"I've phoned her and explained the situation. She's on her way down to you. By the way, best behaviour, three-three; she's furious."

"Yeah, roger-'odge." I did not like the exultant smirk on the guard's face at hearing that last bit. However, I certainly *did* like the way his face fell when the woman in question arrived. It quickly became clear that her ire was directed at *him*, not me. She blasted him with a frosty broadside as I handed her the package. His eyes burned with hatred towards me when she flashed me a smile and signed my docket. They burned even more furiously when I winked at him cheekily.

"Thanks," I called to Mrs Smith as she hurried back towards the lifts. "Cheers mate," I said to the man with the medals with another mischievous wink.

I can't understand why he thought all those horrible expletives would upset me. They only confirmed the scale of my victory. I knew he'd be in a foul mood for the rest of the day whereas I couldn't stop grinning until bedtime.

6: THE KEY WORD IS WEIRD

I must sound a bit conceited or even boastful at times in these books. I can only apologise; but on the other hand, I can only tell it as it was. Believe me, in spite of how smug I sound at times, there were other times when I was a complete and utter... erm... twit, for want of a stronger word.

If you've read, *'You're Where Now?'* you'll know that I've occasionally made a bit of a fool of myself. Chapter 4, *Singing in the Rain*, is a good case in point. Well here's another tale to pop the balloon of my over-inflated ego; although in my defence, dark arts were at work.

Although the weather was still warm, it had been an extremely busy morning but the circuit had thankfully gone very quiet at lunchtime. I'd just completed a drop in Covent Garden so I took the opportunity to slide over to one of my favourite standby plots. A couple of minutes later I was parked up in Irving Street, just off Leicester Square. There were three very good reasons for stopping there. The first was that most welcome, and increasingly rare commodity: a public lavatory (See chapter 7).

There was a motorcycle parking bay beside the loos which was actually my second reason for stopping there. Although traffic wardens would often give us despatchers a couple of minutes' leeway to collect or deliver, they could still get a bit sniffy if you were just sitting there doing nothing on the old double yellows. And it was more than unwelcome to be moved on in the middle of a meal.

Which brings me on to the third reason: the best kebabs in town! There was a kebab joint further up the street towards Leicester square, and its wares were indescribably good. The main reason they stood head and shoulders above every other kebab I've ever eaten was the chilli sauce. It had a rich, rounded flavour that was also hot with a capital 'R' as in, ARGH, my mouth's on fire! Perfect.

"Three-three," I called. The controller answered quickly and readily agreed that I could take a break. I told him exactly where I was just in case a job came across his desk in my location. There was only a one in a million chance it would happen, or even that he'd hang onto it for me if it did. But that was still better odds than the National Lottery, and people buy tickets for that every week.

"Give me a shout when you're ready to roll again," he said in a tone that made it clear that as far as he was concerned, I'd vanished into thin air and was off the board until I'd finished eating. Oh well, at least my kebab was safe.

I put my bike key into my pocket and set off along the road, salivating uncontrollably as I went. I duly bought the object of my desire and wandered back to the bike. At that time it was a gorgeous GS750 Suzuki which drew many an envious glance from my brethren. I hung my lid on one of its mirrors and settled myself onto its seat. Mmm... kebab...

I finished my meal, smoked a JPs, and then got my clipboard out. With pen at the ready I called in.

"That's good timing, three-three; I've got one for you in Charing Cross Road." *I should have bought a lottery ticket.* "Ready for details?"

"Roger."

Brilliant. It was just up the road and was going over to the city - EC2 in fact. That took me right through the heartland of some our best accounts, which meant there was ample opportunity to pick up more jobs on the way. And since I could hear the post-lunch rush coming on strong, there was a good chance that I would. I quickly finished my fag, jumped on the bike, unhooked my helmet and pulled it on. I put my gloves on and went to turn the key. Damn; it was still in my pocket. I ripped my gloves off again and fumbled around in the pockets of my Rukka jacket. I couldn't find it.

I then went through the usual routine. You know the one: check left pocket; it's not there. Check right pocket; it's not there. Check left pocket again; it's not there. Check right pocket again; it's not there. Check... and so on and so forth. Eventually I had to admit defeat – I'd lost it.

Panic set in but I took a long, deep breath and forced myself to stay calm. Clearly I'd dropped it by the bike when I'd put it in my pocket – or missed my pocket as was clearly the case. I looked under the bike, I looked around the bike. I found nothing. The panic came back with a vengeance. This time it took several long, deep breaths to regain some measure of composure. I forced myself to think. Of course, it must have fallen out of my pocket when I'd got my wallet out at the kebab shop. An immense wave of relief washed over me. The fact that said wave was in inverse proportion to the possibility of it actually happening was something that completely escaped me at the time.

Hurriedly, I retraced my steps, carefully studying the ground in case I'd somehow dropped it along the way. It wasn't on the path and neither was it at the shop. I trotted back to the bike – never a good idea in a non-breathable waterproof jacket – and prepared to suffer the indignity of calling in. I could only imagine the torrent of mocking abuse I was about to receive.

Then, just as I was about to transmit my message of shame, I had a clear vision of me opening my jacket and pulling my wallet out from my *inside* pocket. Of course, I'd taken it from there to check whether I had enough cash before going to the shop. I'd then put the wallet in my left jacket pocket. Was it possible that I'd dropped the key into the inside pocket at the same time?

Sweating in anticipation – or was it just the jog from the shop? – I tremblingly reached inside my jacket. I almost sobbed with relief when my fingers touched the little leather fob with its round metal Suzuki badge. In a flash I had it out and rushed to get it into the lock.

There's a good reason for the saying, 'more haste, less speed.' And my 'more haste' did indeed cause 'less speed'. In my rush, I fumbled it and dropped the key. It bounced off the clocks and went who knows where. I definitely heard it clink against the tank though.

"Bugger!" I grunted in frustration. I looked under the bike, I looked around the bike. I found nothing. "Where the hell...?"

I searched and I searched. I looked in all the obvious place, I looked in all the not-so-obvious places. Perhaps it had slid between the headstock and the front of the tank and was sadistically watching my agony from its hiding place there. Nope. Had it performed a mid-air right-angle turn in a parody of Lee Harvey Oswald's magic, president-killing bullet? If so, it could be hiding maliciously on top of the gearbox. Nope.

Ah, of course; it must have slipped through the headstock/tank gap after all, and then made its way to the top of the cylinder head. I got onto my hands and knees and ignoring the apparent impossibility of it all, I peered in. Nothing.

I sat heavily down onto the ground beside the bike and accepted the unlikely reality. Some malignant and supernatural entity had possessed my key and was mercilessly teasing me with it. I hadn't put it in my inside pocket after all. I *had* put it in my left pocket. The vindictive poltergeist had moved it to the inside one just to spite me. It had then snatched it out of my hand and had spirited it away to the bowels of hell.

It says something about the state I'd got myself into that I almost believed it had. Actually, I *knew* it had. So I did the only rational thing I could do under the circumstances: I sparked up a fag. Several years later, this surreal event came clearly to mind when I was once again taunted by malicious evil with my haunted MZ. Another tale related in *'You're Where Now?'*

I swallowed apprehensively and radioed in. To my surprise, the controller wasn't just sympathetic, he was really helpful.

"Hang on there a moment," he said, followed by the general instruction of, "Stand by gents; nobody call."

I waited for a couple of minutes and then the radio squawked into life again.

"Right three-three, there's a place near Primrose Hill called Keys Galore." He quickly gave me their address. "Take a taxi there and they can cut a key for you as long as you've got the key number. Perhaps you've got it written down somewhere. Or if you've got a spare at home, your wife could give you the number. They'll need to see your driving licence though."

"No problem," I said, suddenly overcome with joy. I always had my licence on me – it saved a lot of agro with the law – and the key number was stamped on the lock. I'd always thought it a stupid thing for Suzuki to do, but boy was I glad about it now. "Thanks a lot; I'll be back as soon as I can."

"Roger; good luck."

I pulled out my wallet again. Hmm... by the time I'd paid for the taxi, I probably wouldn't have enough for the key. Electronic payment wasn't yet a reality back then. I was stuck with a two or three mile walk each way. The round journey was going to take a couple of hours plus however long it took to cut the key. I wasn't looking forward to a long hot slog in bike boots, I can tell you.

Then a memory from my past flashed into my mind. A friend from years ago had demonstrated a neat trick with Suzukis when another friend had lost his key. Quite how he'd come by such nefarious knowledge, I have no idea, but if my bike was the same, it would mean I could ride it to Primrose Hill.

I won't give the more light-fingered out there any ideas by telling you how to do it, but it involves a phillips screwdriver and a bent paperclip. I had a paperclip but the screwdriver did present a problem. I'd yet to learn the lesson of being prepared for any eventuality, and my toolkit was under my seat – which I needed the key to open. What I wanted was a rider to return to the bike bay to collect his bike. Then I could...

"Hello, what's this?" A man was standing over at the Garrick theatre waiting to cross the road. And oh joy of joys, he was carrying a crash helmet. He darted across as soon as there was a gap in the traffic and strode purposefully up to the bay. He'd almost reached it when I accosted him.

"'Scuse me, mate, you haven't got a screwdriver I can borrow, have you?"

He looked at me with an expression of distaste. It was only then that I realised he wasn't dressed in bike gear. His light jacket was an expensive-looking, high fashion, cashmere affair while his feet were adorned with rather elegant Chelsea boots. I wondered what his proper bike gear would be like; bloody expensive, obviously. His crash helmet was certainly top of the range. I had a pretty good idea which bike was his as well.

"Why do you need one?" he asked suspiciously in a posh, born-into-money voice.

I explained the reason and waited for his response. He eyed me up and down, clearly reluctant to spoil his never-to-be-used toolkit.

He probably believed that he'd never have to take it from its cubbyhole.

"Please," I implored as pathetically as I could. "It'll save me a *very* long walk."

"Hmm... Okay then; but you'll need to be quick, yah."

I was right. His was the brand spanking new BMW K1000 parked a couple of bikes away from mine.

We'd all scratched our heads in puzzled amazement when this overpriced obscenity had arrived on the market a year or so ago.

"The boxer twins are obsolete and can't be developed any further,' said BMW. "So here's a bang up to date four-cylinder jobbie. Except unlike those uncouth Japs, instead of across the frame, ours will be inline. And instead of the cylinders being boringly upright – or even slanted – our engines will be turned 90 degrees onto their side."

Yep, that was the way forward all right. At least for a couple of years. They then discovered that nobody wanted the 'Brick' as it got labelled. People wanted the old fashioned, horizontally opposed twins because BMW meant boxer. Suddenly, those clever Germans managed to breathe new life into the old design, and it's gone from strength to strength ever since. Meanwhile, the *Brick* sank quietly into the swamp of mediocre oblivion.

So the posh git reluctantly lent me the screwdriver from his BMW toolkit – something that was probably worth more than my bike would cost to replace. He hovered over me as I worked, clearly afraid I would have it on my toes with the blessed instrument. But it was a very quick and easy job and before you could say, 'Oi, come back wiv me bike,' the big GS burst into life. I handed the guy back his screwdriver and thanked him for his generosity. He grunted noncommittedly and watched me all the way as I went up the road. Whether he was admiring my bike or was memorising my number plate, I have no idea. Either option was a good thing as far as I was concerned. Good on yer, mate. If I was nicking the bike, the owner would be damned pleased with his vigilance – although maybe a bit peeved by him lending the thief the means to nick it in the first place!

In no time at all I arrived at Keys Galore and paid the extortionate price for my new key. I didn't care that it was more than twice the price of a normal copy, I was back on the road and I made a fair bit of money that busy afternoon.

But the missing key? Where it went – or even *how* it went – I never found out. It's a mystery as strange as a haunted black MZ...

7: TAKING THE PEE

It's a well-known fact that cold weather causes the human body to piddle more. There's probably a good scientific reason for the phenomenon but what that might be, I don't know. Perhaps a doctor or medical student out there could email me the reason. Whatever the cause, it was a real pain in the backside for us despatch riders. Even cocooned in our best winter bike gear, the cold nipped at our kidneys and pressed on our bladders. Obviously, the warmer you kept, the less often you needed to pee.

There were several problems to be overcome in battling the winter pee-problem. The rapidly disappearing public toilets was one of them, but there was really only one war – and that was the fight to stay warm. There were several solutions but there are three I want to talk about here. Each one had its proponents, and pee-wise, each one had its positives and negatives. The question was: what type of waterproofs should you wear? We wore them every day from mid-autumn to early spring whether it was raining or not.

There were three basic types, the least efficient being the simple jacket and trousers.

They were just as waterproof as the other two but the cold air always found a way in around the waist band. Okay for an hour or two but not all day. In this outfit you were going to need to go often – very often. For me, this was a big no-no.

By far the warmest type (mmm... warmth) was the one-piece. I tried a set once and I have to say they were wicked. I remember one day arriving home, and as I walked through my garden, the ice was cracking and falling off my one-piece like mini icebergs falling into the sea. Inside the suit I was cold, but not dangerously so. As always it was my hands and feet that had suffered most. Consequently, the number of times I'd needed to wet the porcelain was greatly reduced.

The third style though, was my – and indeed, most riders – favoured option: the bib and brace two-piece. To me, it was the perfect compromise.

But why would you want to compromise, I hear you ask. The answer to that is the *need* to pee versus the *ability* to pee. It's a question of access, to put it bluntly.

Imagine the scene; you're busting for a slash but you haven't passed a single public bog for ages. You've got at least another five minutes before you reach your destination. If you're lucky, they might let you use theirs, but...

You start wriggling in your seat, praying to God that you can hang on. As the saying goes, *'There are no atheists in a fox-hole.'*

Then you see it. Praise the lord, a public convenience that's survived Thatcher's cuts. In an instant you're off your bike and running down the steps. Speed becomes even more essential at this point because some great and unfathomable cosmic law has just come into play. This law states that the nearer to the bog you get, the more desperate the urge to pee becomes!

It's best to go to a cubicle if you can, but obviously, that's not always an option. But whether stall, bowl, or trough, the moment of truth has arrived. And here is where your choice of attire comes into play.

Simple jacket and trousers? No problem. Just pull down the waistband and your flies are readily accessed. You may need to go more often, but when you do, it's a cinch.

The bib and brace is more difficult but we experienced boys (I never broached the subject with the few girls in our ranks) had it sussed. Pull your Rukka jacket up as far as you can. Reach up underneath and unclip the bib and brace. Pop the poppers at the side and pull the front down. The braces are elastic so the clips stay in place ready to do up when you're finished. Access to your jeans takes longer and is more restricted than the simple trousers, but the extra hassle is worth it in the end.

Onto the cosy one-piece. Oh dear. Off with your radio and bag; undo your suit; slip your arms out of the sleeves and then pull it all the way down to reveal your jeans. Doesn't take long to say, nor even write, but believe me, when you're doing the, *"I'm about to piss myself!"* war dance, it's an eternity.

Still, whichever style you've chosen, you're now standing before (or sitting on, girls) the font of urinary relief. Now you can relax and let go, right? Wrong. We now approach a point in the tale where those of a gentle disposition might want to skip to the next chapter. I'm about to talk about a cruel affliction only us men have ever suffered. My friends referred to it as, 'D. R. Dick'.

The logistics of taking a wiz now present a daunting obstacle. You not only have to get your old chap out of your flies, you've got to pee *past* your pulled down waterproofs. And you're more than likely wearing long johns or tights (yes, tights were often worn) as well. This would be tricky enough at the best of times, but we know what happens to the old fellow when he gets cold, don't we lads. So the poor little feller's got further to go with less length to get there. Without the greatest of care, the result could be a disaster! Far, far worse than had you not spotted the loo in the first place – if you get my meaning.

There was one company I worked for that had a brilliant poster on the riders' room wall. It was a Peanuts cartoon with the words 'dark' replaced by 'waterproof'. Charlie brown was lamenting that, *"Doing a good job here is like wetting yourself in waterproof trousers; you get a nice warm feeling but nobody notices."*

I'm here to tell you that truer words have never, ever been spoken.

8: TOURISTS

Ah, those long hot summers back in the day. Perhaps it's a trick of the memory but it really does seem that they were somehow... better. Still, it could just be the rose coloured specs and all that. Nostalgia hasn't dampened my ire about the lack of work though. It was devastating to the family finances; but that's a subject I've touched on more than once so I'll drop it – for now, anyway.

As well as keeping warm and dry summer did have other compensations to mitigate the impact of financial ruin. Sunbathing, for instance. Many a rider would strip off his shirt and use his bike as a sunbed. It sounds tricky to the uninitiated but it's quite easy to do. Sit on the seat the wrong way round and just lay back with your head on the clocks. Put your jacket or your bag there first though – you need a nice comfy pillow. Always an idea to make sure your tank hasn't got too hot by the way, or you'll shoot back upright with a loud expletive on your lips. Best to lay your tee-shirt across it first.

It wasn't unusual to fall asleep like this, which you'd think would pose a problem if you *were* actually called into action. The thing is, if you were parked up at one of the more frequented stand-by haunts, you'd usually find two or three colleagues from your own company there.

A quick, "How long you been here?" would give you a pretty good idea of how long you'd have to wait for your turn to come up. And unless some joker wanted to play a prank on you, the last to go would give you a nudge to let you know you were now on your own.

But what if you were on your own from the start? What if you dozed off in the heat, wafted away to night-night land by the soporific lullaby of the passing traffic? For an experienced rider, that wasn't a problem. It was also the reason I always strived to keep the same call sign. You see, your ear got 'tuned in' to hearing it. If you were blatting along, and the radio chatter was just an unintelligible chirruping behind the rush of wind noise, you could still somehow hear your own number. It just seemed to rise up above the roar and gently tap you on your shoulder. And it was the same when you were dozing. Those two words, "Three-three," would jerk me back to the real world like an electric shock; most of the time, anyway.

But apart from catching some rays, there was other entertainment available. Okay, not so much if you were on your own, but when there was half a dozen of you, it could be a real laugh. Football with a crash helmet; scoring the passing hotties out of ten; or somewhat cruelly, giving directions to tourists.

There were strict rules to this particular game, and as in a lot of games, there were winners and losers. Unfortunately, the winners or losers were the tourists themselves. Asked nicely, they always got good directions from us; and believe me, a long term courier was as good, if not better than a black cab driver. If they weren't polite they'd get a blank faced, "Dunno mate, I'm new around here." If the enquirer was downright rude or arrogant on the other hand, they'd get clear and precise instructions with no need to ask anyone else along the way. Unfortunately for them, they would be in completely the wrong direction. A nasty thing to do, admittedly. And now I'm older and wiser, it's something of which I'm very much ashamed. You have to admit though, there was a touch of poetic justice to it.

"Serves 'em bloody well right. Might teach 'em some manners," we often said.

Funnily enough, the cruellest game would be played with our American cousins. Now American tourists have long been stereotyped as loud, brash, and abrasive. Stereotypes are usually pretty baseless, but this one was often uncannily accurate. And they definitely drew the shortest of straws. Many, if not most, however, were polite and respectful. So clearly they automatically got proper instructions, right? Wrong! They still had one more hoop to jump through, and not many of them managed it. It all had to do with pronunciation.

"Excuse me son, can you tell me how to get to LIE-SESTER square?" Or how about, "BURK-LEE Square?" or worst of all, "GROSS-VEN-NOR

Square?" What? Your own embassy's there and you can't even say it right?

"Yeah mate. Go straight up Regent Street till you come to the big road – that's Marylebone road; turn right, keep on and it's on your right opposite a big train station." Oh how we chuckled; oh how I go red with shame at the thought of it now. What a heartless bastard I was. But then again, some of us saw it as pay back for the treatment we received if we had to go to the US Embassy in said GROSS-VEN-NOR Square. For the record, I'd like to point out to my many American chums (if they haven't just crossed me off their Christmas card list) it's Grosvenor Square which is pronounced 'Grove-ner' Square. Berkeley Square is 'Barkley' and of course, LIE-SESTER is Leicester pronounce 'Lester'.

In spite of the rude and sometimes threatening way your embassy people treated us despatch riders, I cannot apologise enough to all those otherwise nice Americans who found themselves scratching their heads opposite Euston Station. It was unforgivable; I'm sorry; I'm very sorry.

And in the same way, to the rest of you – I mean *all* the others whether British, French,

German, or Martian; all of you who were rude, obnoxious, and arrogant visitors to our great capital in the eighties; to all of you I also apo...aplo...apple...appello... Hmm, it seems sorry really *is* the hardest word.

9: TYRED OUT

Bikers all over the world belong to a kind of brotherhood. Always have and probably always will. But within that brotherhood we still tend to be somewhat tribal. There are those who prefer Suzuki's over Yamaha's – or vice versa. Some like the latest incarnation of the Triumph brand while other, more traditionalist-minded riders think the last *real* Triumph was the '74 T150 Trident or the '69 T120R Bonneville. And even then there'll be fierce arguments about which of the two is the best. At least now the two-stroke versus four-stroke debate has been put to bed – unless like me, you're into classic Japanese bikes of course!

My point is, whenever a bunch of bikers get together, it doesn't take long for some kind of earnest debate to start over something or another. And we despatch riders were together a lot and we had more than most to argue about. On top of the usual stuff, we had the added differences over what bike was best suited to our job. Big or small, shaft drive or chain, two-stroke or four-stroke. There were other disagreements too, but I think the one that got most airtime was what tyre was best.

The main contenders for a while were Michelin and Avon. I'd always liked the AM21/23 Avon Roadrunner myself. Apparently you can still get them, so they can't have been too bad. They were my preferred tyres because they lasted well and had a reasonable amount of grip. They might not have stuck to the road as well as some others, but they always gave you good warning when they were about to let go. A lot of the grippier tyres – particularly Metzeler Lazers which later became fashionable – tended to grip and grip, and then bang; you were sliding up the road on your arse. The Avon was to my mind a very good compromise.

I was once persuaded to buy a Michelin back tyre – and only once, might I add. Normally I'd have stuck to my trusty Roadrunners, but not only did my friends rave about the grip of this particular bit of rubber, it was in the shop at a knock-down price! How could I refuse? I should have known better.

I bought it (I have no memory of exactly which Michelin it was) on the Saturday and fitted it to my blue Suzuki GS400 as part of its routine weekend maintenance. A quick Sunday afternoon blatt soon had it nicely scrubbed in ready for work. Just as well because Monday arrived and it was hammering down with rain. I set off for town gingerly trying to get the feel of the new rubber's wet weather performance. I will concede that I was pleasantly surprised. It gripped really well and definitely seemed as predictable as the Avon it had replaced – in the wet at least.

I got my first job fairly quickly. It was a not very nice Covent Garden going Kennington. I say not very nice simply because there was little chance of anything else going that way, and even less chance of a pick up to bring me back in. And the dreaded "Back this way" would mean joining the last of the rush hour crawl across Waterloo Bridge; yippee.

I'd only got as far as the Elephant and Castle when I got the first puncture.

"Damn," I said, probably using somewhat stronger language. I guessed I must have pinched the tube slightly when I'd fitted it. It was something I hadn't done for many years now, but anything was possible. When I had the tyre off and checked it though, it was clear that I'd picked up a nail.

It didn't take long to put a patch on the tube and set off again. I did a couple of jobs and then just as I was filtering past a line of cars, the back end suddenly stepped out, almost catching me off-guard.

"Bugger! Not another one."

This time it was more than possible I'd pinched the tube, but far more likely that my patch had simply lifted. After all, mending a puncture while sitting at the side of a busy road in the pouring rain isn't ideal. But again any doubts concerning my workmanship proved groundless. It was another flaming nail! I went through the tiresome (pun not intended) routine again and resumed work.

It seemed to have been just an unlucky coincidence as all went well until mid-afternoon. But then – you guessed it – another bloody nail through my brand new sodding Michelin! This was getting spooky.

"Three-three, I've got *another* flaming puncture!" I lamented over the radio.

For once it was my controller who suggested that I go home. "Change that tyre!" he instructed forcefully. "It must be defective or something."

"Roger, will do." Like hell I would! The thought of telling the wife that I needed *another* new tyre just two days after buying this one wasn't something I relished. Especially as there'd been some tension between us about having to spend money on "that bloody bike" in the first place. And anyway, I reasoned hopefully, no amount of defects could cause a tyre to attract nails like a magnet. No, I'd just fit a new tube and give it a really good checking over. Three punctures in one day just *had* to be bad luck!

Next day, I set off with everything properly fitted and checked. I was actually looking forward to work for once. It had been pretty busy lately and if I played my cards right, I could earn a fair bit. That would go some way towards making up for yesterday's fiasco.

I didn't even make it into town before I had my next puncture. This was getting beyond a joke! It took me forever to find exactly what had caused it this time. It certainly wasn't a nail – that would have been far too easy. In fact, I couldn't identify the object at all when it eventually came to light. All I can say is that it was long, very thin, and incredibly sharp. It looked more like a needle than anything else. It left such a tiny hole in the tube, it was almost impossible to find. But find it I did in the end.

I repaired the tube with the last patch from my now empty puncture outfit and turned back towards home. I rode slowly and carefully, all the way praying that I didn't pick up another nail, needle – or sodding Bowie knife come to that! I needn't have worried though, because bike and rider arrived safely home. Of course 'safely' is a relative term. The row that ensued when *she who must be obeyed* learned of my intentions to ditch the Michelin was explosive. Still, it wasn't unexpected, and neither was it unique. It happened every time I had this sort of problem.

"No; we can't afford it," she snapped furiously. She was right, we couldn't.

"We can't afford not to," I countered, also getting angry. I was right, we couldn't.

"It's a brand new tyre! It must be just coincidence." She was right, it must be. The colour of her eyes always changed according to her mood, and since they were now green, it meant that I was in extreme danger. But I persisted anyway.

"Brand new or not, I've had four punctures in two days. That's more than I've had in the last two years!" I was right, it was.

"We haven't got the money in the bank!" she screamed. She was right, we hadn't.

"So what the hell am I supposed to do then?" I shouted back. "I can't keep getting punctures!" I was right, I... oh you get the idea.

In the end, a compromise was agreed. I would put my knackered AM21 back on – but only until the weekend. Maybe I could push it for another week, but that really would be sailing close to the wind. It was a fag-paper's width away from a fine and a CU30 on my licence already; and If I got too many distance jobs...

As it was I bought a new Avon that very weekend; and you know what? It lasted 8,000 miles and in all that time, I never suffered a single puncture. As a footnote I'd like to add that when this blessed tyre reached its wear-bars, circumstances were such that I had to revert to that accursed Michelin. To my immense surprise, it didn't get a single puncture – for one day at least. By midmorning on the second day, I was again sitting by the side of the road. This time I didn't have to patch it, I'd learned a lesson that was to stay with me for the rest of my despatching days. This time I had a brand new inner tube in my panniers – along with all manner of other stuff. The lesson I'd learned was: *BE PREPARED!*

10: THE LONGEST DAY

As you've no doubt gathered by now, being a London despatch rider was a job of wildly varying extremes. You could spend days– or even weeks – sitting around in penury-inducing boredom, or you could be charging around, totally stressed out as you try to cope with more work than you could possibly juggle. In summer you could find yourself sweating it out between the cars and buses in stratospheric temperatures. They went off the scale of my friend's thermometer during one particularly hot spell. But in winter you were constantly battling hypothermia – even frostbite on one occasion. And of course, there was the money. It varied like the tides and the seasons. And the hours? Don't get me started. Oh all right then; if you insist, I will.

Every now and then you'd get a nice early finish but would still have earned a reasonable day's pay. Those days were made all the sweeter by their rarity. On the whole though, you were expected to be on circuit – in town ready and waiting for work – for around ten hours a day, five days a week. In reality, what with sickies and breakdowns, most riders only managed to average four days. But from leaving home in the morning to arriving home at night, the working day was usually twelve hours, give or take. There was, however, one day that was particularly gruelling.

It was mid-November and the weather was cold but pleasantly dry and bright. My machine of choice at the time was a Kawasaki GT550. It was a company bike that was painted a horrid and uninspiring green. It did have a very useful handlebar fairing, however. I'd had the privilege of getting an early morning booking in Stratford, E15. The pickup was booked for 8:30 am and it was going all the way up to Milton Keynes. A nice sixty-mile run.

All went well with the job and I dropped the parcel off at around nine-thirty. By being a bit heavy on the throttle I managed to be back in the thick of it by ten-forty-five. I had thirty-odd quid in my bin which was a good half day's pay already. And since it was Friday, it was also payday. Things were really looking bright.

It was reasonably busy all morning – nothing spectacular, but I did manage to bag a Slough, which was always a nice little run. All in all, it was a nice steady pace, and that was exactly the way I liked it. The only disappointment was that I hadn't managed to pass the office to grab my wages.

As expected, it went quiet around lunchtime which meant time for a nice quiet bite to eat. Unlike most Fridays, however, it was very slow to get going in the afternoon. Still, I thought, I mustn't be greedy. By two-fifteen I'd already bagged at least sixty quid, so I didn't really care if it was as dead as a dodo until home time.

"Three-three, three-three" the controller called.

"Yeah, three-three," I replied, my pen at the ready.

"Get me on the phone, on the phone." All controllers tended to repeat the *"on the phone"* instruction.

Hmm... There were only a couple of possibilities here. Either I was about to get a rollicking for something I'd done wrong or I was about to be given a plum. I quickly found a phone box and rung in.

"Yeah, it's three-three; I was asked to ring in," I told the telephonist.

"Hi; John said you'd call. Hang on a mo."

Good, she sounded pretty cheerful. I was fairly sure a rollicking was off the cards. Unless something I'd done just needed clarifying, I was definitely getting something good.

"Hi Stephen, how're you feeling?"

Hmm; he used my name and not my call sign. And why the concern for my welfare?

"I'm okay thanks; why?" I asked warily.

"Fancy a run out?"

"Yes," I said, even more suspicious of where this was going. Why on earth would he ask? "Where am I going?" I probed suspiciously.

"Liverpool."

My heart skipped a beat. Had I just heard right? A job going more than two hundred miles? This sort of thing wasn't unheard of but it was extremely rare. A lot of the riders who'd done these runs had taken the train while leaving their bikes parked at the station. When they'd arrived, they'd simply jumped into a taxi to finish the job. It sounds crazy today when trains are so expensive that it's cheaper to fly, but back then, the fare was very affordable. It was the taxi ride that could put a spanner in the financial works. They just had to hope that the drop was near to the station.

People will often tell you how bad the trains were before they were privatised. They cite the workers' bad attitude, the stale sandwiches in the buffet car, and the filthy, old-fashioned trains. All of which is true, of course, but there's no point in having whizz-bang pristine rolling stock if you can't afford to ride in them, is there? Personally, I'd rather sit in a dirty, obsolete train than admire an immaculate, state of the art one flashing past if I can't afford to ride in it. I love top of the range, prestige cars as much as anyone, but imagine if they were the only ones in the showroom.

"Lovely cars you've got here mate, but you haven't got anything that fits my bank balance. I guess I'll just have to catch a bus."

Still, despite the affordability of the train ride, I always said that I'd use the bike if one of these plummiest of plums came my way.

"Brilliant! Where's the pickup?" I enquired enthusiastically.

"Goswell road." He went on to give me the full details. "Call me pee-oh-bee."

I hung up and drew a deep breath. This was going to be the longest run I'd ever done. The furthest I'd ever been was the Welsh border or Birmingham – and of course, Poole; none of which were much more than a hundred and twenty miles. This was going to be almost double that; plus the return, of course. God knows what time I'd get home. I quickly phoned the wife to let her know I was going to be late; *very* late.

"Wow, that's good," she said happily. "Be careful though, it's a long way."

"I will," I assured her, surprised and delighted by her concern. "Trouble is, I won't be able to grab my wage packet till Monday." I held my breath and waited for the bomb to go off. The prospect of a weekend without money might be too much for her.

"That's okay. It'll be worth it when you get next week's wages." Her tone changed to one of concern. "Have you got enough on you for the journey?"

"I should have plenty. I did a couple of cash jobs yesterday." True enough, I'd pulled in a good twenty quid's worth of 'sausage' (rhyming slang, as in *sausage and mash – cash*) the day before. Added to that, I still had some of my week's petrol allowance left.

With her indoors' 'good luck' ringing in my ears, I shot round to the pickup.

"No real rush," the man said as he handed me the large jiffy bag. "Just so long as it's there by six-ish."

"No problem," I said reassuringly. I then hurried down to the bike, lit up a smoke and called in as instructed.

"Away you go three-three. Phone me empty."

"Roger-'odge." After a few deep puffs I stamped out my cigarette and then swung a leg over the bike. I felt a tingle of excitement as I fired up the Kwacker. This was going to be an adventure that would push me to my limits. And I was about to find out just where those limits could be found.

It was an easy enough journey on the face of it. Straight up Goswell road, follow the A1 up to Brent Cross and pick up the M1. Eighty miles further on you branch off onto the M6 and follow it virtually the whole rest of the way. Simples. Hah!

I threaded my way through the traffic, which being Friday, was already beginning to get heavy as it flowed out of the capital. Eventually, I hit the motorway and settled into the big, comfy seat. I kept the speed down below the seventy limit since there was little point in wasting fuel by going faster. And anyway, there was too much traffic in the way to give the GT its head.

A leisurely fuel stop (and ubiquitous cigarette) thirty miles later set me up for the rest of the journey north. Once again I joined the motorway and tucked down behind the fairing.

It was something of a novelty to have a fairing to keep the wind and weather off you back then. To be honest, I'd always regarded them as being something for wimps. Real men liked to feel the force of the wind on their body. Rain and snow? Hah, I laugh in their face! If you've read *'You're Where Now?'* you'll know that laughing was the last thing I now felt like doing. I found myself really appreciating the big stingray attached to the bars in front of me, but I didn't realise just how much I'd appreciate it later on.

By now the traffic had thinned out and I let the speed edge up slightly – but only slightly. As frugal as the GT550 was, I still had to bear in mind the bike's range. Yes, it was a big tank but you never know. I glanced at the clock on the fairing (actually a cheap and strapless Casio watch that I'd glued on with a sticky pad) and grinned. I was making pretty good time. About forty-five minutes later I turned onto the M6.

I don't know why but I had the impression that London was the only city that had a really bad rush hour. That illusion was now shattered into a zillion pieces. It was nearly half-past-four and I was still a few miles from the outskirts of Birmingham when things went all pear-shaped. The motorway was packed solid as though there'd been an accident up ahead. I decided that had to be the answer because I was heading *towards* the city which meant the road should have been virtually empty. I've since discovered that this sort of traffic jam was then a regular occurrence – hence the opening of the M6 toll road in 2003.

Now in my humble opinion, the Kawasaki GT550 was one of – if not *the* – the best despatch bike of them all. It was quick, frugal, and bulletproof. It was extremely comfortable on a long journey too. It wasn't as nimble through heavy traffic as a true lightweight though. And the blessing of that fairing now became something of a curse. I suppose it shouldn't have made a difference; after all, it didn't restrict lock, and nor did it add any width to speak of. I truly believe it was simply that it restricted visibility – or perhaps it was just psychological. But for whatever the reason, I was having real trouble threading my way through the bumper to bumper motorway crawl. I consoled myself with the thought that it couldn't go on for too long.

The miles inched past and the time crept by. It was by now dark and still the congestion refused to clear. I wrestled the portly beast through gaps; I squeezed between the long lines of cars as I filtered through them. My mind was the only thing moving with any speed. It was racing as I concentrated on the twinkling red tail lights of the jammed up crawl in front of me. Unfortunately these made visibility even worse; the brightly shining rubies distorted and glared through the screen while the frequent flashes of the many brake lights blinded and disorientated me.

It went on and on and by now I was exhausted. Not until at least an hour later did it begin to open up. Frustratingly, as so often happens in this type of jam, there was no apparent reason for the snarl-up; it just ended. And in all that time I'd covered little more than ten miles! It was now a quarter to six and I still had the best part of a hundred miles to go. The parcel was already going to be late, and to make things worse, I now needed to make a fuel stop and have a pee-break. Fortunately, the next services came up almost immediately and there I hurriedly went through the motions. I smoked my ciggie as I walked briskly to the loos before filling the bike's tank to the brim. Unbelievably quickly, I was back on the bike and away.

To my amazement the motorway was now uncannily deserted. It was as if some unseen force had cleared my path and was saying, "There you are, Muir; go for it!" And go for it I did. With a bellow of gratitude, the ugly brute beneath me opened its stride and galloped up to ninety. I kept a careful eye out for the little laybys where the plod liked to sit, quietly waiting to pounce on a speeding car or bike. They were like spiders waiting patiently for a fly to stray onto their web.

Despite that, every now and then the frustration of missing my deadline would get too much for me. Every now and then I pinned the throttle against the stop. I'd tuck in behind the screen and watch the speedo needle nudge a hundred and fifteen. Not bad for a shaft-driven tourer.

I'm proud to say it was just under an hour later when I cruised into the outskirts of Liverpool. Of course, I had no idea of where I needed to go but as usual, I followed my nose and looked for someone to ask for directions. There was nobody. Apart from some light traffic, Liverpool seemed to be a ghost town. Eventually though, I spotted a couple of boys playing on a bit of grass about thirty yards away from the road.

"Oi," I shouted as I pulled the bike up near them. "Here a minute."

The lads looked over at me and then put their heads together. After a few seconds of discussion, they nodded to each other and wandered cautiously over.

They were scruffy little ten-year old oiks and they eyed the GT enviously. "That's a cool bike mister; gissa go." His thick, scouse accent came straight out of Brookside.

"Sorry son, I'm in a hurry." I ignored his disappointed scowl and went on to ask for directions.

"Oh that's easy. I'll get on the back of your bike and show you."

"Yeah, there's loads of room; we could both fit on," his mate added.

"I tell you what, you tell me how to get there and I'll take you for a spin when I've dropped off my parcel."

It took some doing to persuade them both that I would come back, but in the end they relented and told me where to go. Once again my nose had led me in roughly the right direction. If the boys were being truthful, I was less than a mile from the drop-off. Five minutes later I did indeed arrive. A security guard had to sign for the package since the place was now shut for the weekend. Either the intended recipient would come back for it later on, or it would sit there until Monday. Whatever the case, late or not, I'd done my job. I could now go home.

After using the guard's toilet I wandered back out to the bike and – you guessed it – sparked up a fag. It was only then that it hit me just how knackered I really was. And not only was I knackered, I was bloody cold. I made a quick calculation in my head. No flaming wonder I was clapped out; I'd done the best part of four hundred miles already that day! My heart sank to my boots as I realised I still had more than two hundred to go. I could have cried, but real men don't do that, do they?

"Ah well," I said resignedly as I stamped out my ciggie. "A journey not started is one not completed." I grinned. "That's a good line S P, you should put that in a book. Twenty five years later I did just that when I wrote *'The Talisman of Wrath'*.

I set off again on the downhill stretch and soon spotted the two lads waiting for me. They'd crossed the road so as to be on my side and were waving frantically. Unfortunately, I couldn't see them since I was straining my head trying to spot them where they'd originally been. I even stood up on the foot pegs in an effort to locate them. Shame they weren't there, tee-hee.

Once out onto the M6 again, I cruised along at a sensible seventy, unsure of how much fuel I had. The 550's gauge had a mind of its own. Fortuitously, the poor thrashed beastie spluttered onto reserve about ten miles short of a services. Just made it. Boy had my thrashing guzzled fuel! I took the opportunity to have another pee and a smoke, and then I was away again. About an hour later it began to rain. Not heavily, mind, and looking at the sky I reckoned I'd soon be clear of it, but it certainly made me feel even colder.

The miles thundered by and as they disappeared into my mirrors, so did my energy reserves. And as I neared the end of my endurance, the cold bit deeper and deeper. Two of my despatch buddies had been in this situation and both had succumbed to the cold and exhaustion. Both of them had lost consciousness and come off their bikes. One had been lucky enough to go sliding down the middle lane, breaking his arm in the process. The other, however, had tangled with the central reservation's armco. The accident had torn off the poor chap's left leg below the knee. Impressively though, this little hero had returned to work once he'd recovered. He simply used the heel off his prosthetic leg to change up. Chapeau, my friend; chapeau.

The memory of their tales demanded some kind of action. I needed to stop and warm up. Food would be a good idea too! As tempting as the thought of sitting in a service station's Burger King was, the lure of home was far greater. In the end I decided just to stop for another pee and a fag.

Once again the speedo needle crept clockwise. Seventy became seventy-five, then eighty, and then beyond. The broken white lines flashed hypnotically past in the shining bright pool of my headlight beam. Were it not for the deep chill in my bones, I know I would have given in to the call of sleep. Then up ahead I saw the lights of that most blessed of oasis', a services.

I swept up the slip road and parked as close to the entrance as I could. Leaping from the bike I promptly crumpled to the ground. I was that far gone. Cursing furiously I managed to climb unsteadily to my feet. The way I staggered toward the loos, a watching policeman would have breathalysed me on the spot! Luckily, there wasn't one around.

I made it to the toilets and went through the ridiculous, 'find-the-shrivelled-penis' routine. I then had the bright idea of holding my frozen hands under the hot tap. It was delicious! It was when I was drying them off in the blower that I had an even brighter idea. I crouched beneath it using it like a fan heater. Not a very efficient fan heater, but a welcome stream of warm air nonetheless. Sighing happily, I pulled out my box of ciggies. I let out a horrified gasp; there was only one solitary fag left rattling around in it now. How had I not noticed before? I would have to find somewhere in the service complex to buy some more.

A dreadful fear suddenly washed over me. With trembling hands I pulled out my wallet and opened it.

"Shit, shit, shit!" I cried in dismay. There wasn't enough left to buy any. Even if I *had* wanted to grab a burger, I didn't possess the funds. I closed my eyes and did a quick calculation in my head. Miles left, about a hundred. How much fuel was left in that huge tank? Nope, not a clue. I'd have to take a look when I got back to the bike. A sense of panic welled up inside me, but I managed to force it down. Another of the GT550's qualities was the size of its tank – it was huge. I was sure there'd be enough if I took it steady. Hah! Fat chance of that.

I pulled out my last precious cigarette, slid out of the warm air flow, and lit it. I drew the wondrous smoke deep into my lungs and blew it out in a long, satisfying stream. God it tasted good. I haven't touched a cigarette for more than twenty years now, and just the thought of them sends a disgusted shudder through my body. Even so, I still remember that particular smoke with a kind of nostalgic love. It was the best one of my life.

Every few seconds I had to reach up and wave my hand around the dryer's sensor to activate it again; something which began to get rather tiresome. I drew some strange looks from the (thankfully few) men who came into the loo, I can tell you. One of them had the temerity to wash his hands and I had to move aside so he could dry them. Was that anger in his eyes or anxiety? He certainly had some stones to approach a filthy, wild-looking biker who was clearly some kind of nutter. To be honest, I was far too wrapped up in my own misery to care.

I smoked my fag all the way down to the filter and then glanced at my watch. It must have gained somehow. There was no way it was quarter to ten!

I stumbled back to the bike and swung my leg over. Flipping open the filler cap and peering inside I swung the bike from side to side. A wave of relief flooded my body. I blessed Mr Kawasaki – if such a man existed – for providing the bike with such a wondrous fuel capacity. There was still plenty of go-juice swishing around inside.

I fired it up and headed for the exit. The engine howled eagerly as I accelerated back onto the motorway. The speedo hardly dropped below eighty-five as I pounded the tarmac and concrete towards my goal. Although the fairing provided some welcome protection against the hurricane blast of icy wind, it did present a problem that grew with every mile I covered. It channelled the deflected slipstream in such a way that it caught the top of my helmet. This pounded against it, rattling my head from side to side alarmingly. It was no wonder I'd fallen over when I'd got off the bike. If I tried ducking below the blast, I was looking through the screen. This distorted the view at the best of times, but it was now also extremely dirty. At this speed it was positively suicidal, so I had no choice but to endure the helmet-battering all the way home.

I'd been somewhat refreshed by my toilet-stop, but pretty soon fatigue became a problem again. At the very next services I repeated the hand-dryer trick, and the one after that too. The lack of nicotine at these stops was pure torture though. In the end it was way past eleven o'clock when I tumbled through the front door and into the arms of my wife. She guided me to an armchair and sat me down. I ponced a fag off her and sat there drawing on its life-giving smoke before even thinking about removing my gear. By the time I'd finished it there was a steaming cup of coffee on the little table beside me.

I'm warming your dinner up. It won't be long," said saint wife, the blessed provider of comfort and sustenance. At least that's who she was at that moment in time.

I took a deep breath and then removed my filthy boots and bike gear. Wearily I went to the downstairs cloakroom for a quick wash. Tomorrow I'd have a bath, but tonight? Just dinner and bed – and of course, exhausted though sweet dreams about the week's wages I'd earned in this one single day; this one longest of all those long days.

11: WORKHORSES

Several people have requested that I include a chapter about those unsung heroes of the despatch rider's life – the bikes. Which one was the best? Which ones were the most popular? Which ones were the worst?

Since I've personally owned or used at least thirty different models for despatching, I think I can answer those questions fairly accurately. Okay, my opinion will be highly subjective; let's face it, many a fierce argument was had amongst us on this very topic. Some liked the bigger bikes' out of town performance advantage, where I much preferred a smaller bike's in-town manoeuverability. That was after all, where I spent most of my time. As you can imagine, practically every bike on the market was used by someone at some time and there are far too many to list here.

These then are *my* views on some of the bikes most commonly used.

Kawasaki GT550: As I said in the previous chapter, I consider this to be the best of all the despatch riders' bikes. I did a lot of miles on these beasties but never actually owned one myself. It was used as company bikes by some of the top notch outfits such as Addison Lee. It was quicker than the overweight CX500 and had a better fuel consumption as well. The engine could reach a stratospherically high mileage before any major repairs became necessary. It was wonderfully comfortable too.

It did have a couple of flaws though, but these were minor and only really came to light after a good few thousand hard miles. The two main problems were the suspension and the front discs. The former was always the first problem to raise its ugly head in the shape of the failure of the air assisted suspension. Quite simply, the air sacks inside them would burst. This was usually due to being overinflated at one time or another, which was easily done without the proper inflator. Since repair or replacement was expensive, most riders just left them busted and put up with the soggy handling when the bike was pushed hard.

The problem with the discs was their rapid rate of wear. All despatch bikes' front brakes took a hammering, but for some reason the GT's discs seemed to get wafer thin quicker than most. The pads also had a higher than average rate of wear, and the discs seemed a little more expensive to replace than most.

As I said, these were high-mileage problems that don't really detract from what was a damn fine, if rather boring-looking (ugly?) motorcycle.

Honda CX500: Ah, the good old Plastic Maggot. Was there ever an uglier, more ridiculously engined motorcycle ever built? Probably not, but it did a fine job as a despatch bike all the same. It's still probably the one most associated with the industry and I certainly covered fair few miles on them. When it first came out though, it had a ludicrous number of teething troubles, mostly related to the cam chain. "The what?" I hear you cry. "You're a moron, S P; the CX's engine was overhead valve; it had push rods, not a cam chain." And in a way you're right; it *is* OHV and it *does* have push rods. But that's one of the reasons it's such a ridiculous engine.

For some strange reason, Honda always seemed to have had difficulties with their cam chains and/or tensioners. That's one of the reasons why the final incarnation of the VFR750 ended up without a single chain in the whole bike! But some bright spark at Honda one day said, "I know, we'll build an OHV, vee twin; and just so we get the worst of both worlds, we'll give it a cam chain as well. And even better, we'll bury said chain so deep in the bowels of the engine, it'll need a complete – and overwhelmingly expensive – strip down to get at it." Hmm...

Still, once the teething troubles were sorted, the CX was an incredibly reliable mount. It was much used by the companies that rented bikes to us couriers. It was fat and a bit top heavy but certainly had many fine attributes. It was smooth and comfortable, but personally, in spite of the miles I covered on them (or *because* of those miles) I hated the bloody things.

Honda VT500: Another Honda vee twin but a much better bet. It was lighter and more agile than either the CX or the GT, and it was quicker than the Kawasaki too. It didn't seem to be quite as bulletproof though. Even so, if well maintained, they could put on some extremely impressive high mileages. I really liked them although sadly, I only ever had one, and that only for a short time.

Suzuki GS425: I liked these. They were as tough as old boots and much smaller than the shaft driven 500 class bikes. Obviously, they weren't nearly as quick, but 40 bhp was more than enough round town. I used a company 425 once but actually *owned* the earlier GS400 version. Both would just about touch a ton and were reasonably inexpensive to run. In 1983 they were superseded by the next bike on my list.

Suzuki GSX400: I talked about this one in earlier chapters. The main difference between the GS and the GSX engines was the cylinder head. The boring old GS's four valve head was replaced by an eight valve job on the GSX. This gave it four ponies more than the 425 – a full ten percent! It ran a lot leaner too giving it an impressive fuel consumption, even around town.

Apparently, the eight valve head caused a lot of problems, but I never had any trouble with mine. The only real bugbear was something the entire Suzuki GSX range had trouble with – crap alternators. The windings on the stator burnt out so regularly, they kept one particular auto electrics shop going for years! But engine-wise, mine was brilliant. The thing handled pretty well too. I did more than seventy thousand miles on it with only those electrical bugbears to contend with. We parted company when I crashed into a U-turning Volvo (see *'You're Where Now?'* chapter 8)

Incidentally, a year or so after I'd crashed it I saw it back on the road going over Chelsea Bridge. I immediately spun around and chased it down. The rider obligingly pulled over and we had a bit of a chat. It turned out that the damage had been mostly cosmetic and it had now done well over a hundred thousand miles. It was still on its original cam chain (Honda take note) and even more amazingly, it still had its original clutch! Admittedly the plates were by now completely knackered and were slipping uncontrollably, but even so... Also, the bike smoked heavier than I did and struggled to hit ninety, - but it was still running! Oh how I miss that game little twin.

Honda CB250RS: What a cracker of a bike this was. It shouldn't have worked, but it did. It's also hard to believe that it came from the same manufacturer that gave us such an overweight porker as the CX. What happened over in Tokyo when it was conceived? The appalling lard-arsed two-fifty Superdream (sorry guys, but it *was* pretty awful) was inexplicably selling in bucket loads. But a year later they brought out this completely different concept to run as the indifferent but hugely popular twin's stablemate.

The RS was small, nimble, and although having just one solitary cylinder, it was only one gee-gee shy of the Superdream's twenty-seven. Its diminutive proportions therefore gave it a massive advantage in the power-to-weight ratio stakes. This made it not only quick but economical to boot. It handled really well too.

Around town it was brilliant, and it could hold seventy all day long on the open road. A diligently serviced RS could keep going reliably for forty thousand plus miles. Even then, a top-end rebuild was a doddle. I've had several of them.

There were, however, a couple of irritations to contend with, but then again, show me a bike that's perfect and I'll eat my crash hat! Firstly, it devoured final drive chains at a terrifying rate. A standard chain needed adjusting twice a day when it was busy. It would be totally knackered before you'd finished your breakfast! Even a heavy duty O-ring chainset would be chewed up quicker than almost any other bike on the market. Why? I haven't the foggiest.

The other thing to watch out for was the oil level. The engine only had a small sump capacity which overworked your 10w40 mercilessly, which in turn caused it to simply evaporate. It was imperative to check it every morning and I even had to top it up during the day once or twice. An early engine demise was almost always due to the oil level dropping too low. Keep a wary eye on it, and you've got yourself one of the best local bikes on the circuit.

Honda CD200 Benly: On the face of it the Benly was an absurd choice for a despatch rider. Only four gears, soggy suspension, and a top whack of 80mph (on a good day) made it a totally impractical mount. Almost all the big outfits refused to employ anyone with a bike below 250cc anyway, so your choice of employer was severely limited. Added to that were the howls of derisive mirth you'd have to endure from your sensibly-mounted fellows. But if you could put up with all that, the little 200 did provide some real benefits. I sang its praises in *'You're Where Now?'* but here's a reminder of them anyway.

First of all, it was small and nimble. It could wriggle through gaps that stymied the portly CX's that so many riders favoured. And despite those diminutive proportions, the seat was huge and extremely well padded – essential for a long day in the saddle. The 80mph top whack did make it a drag on the motorway or fast A roads, but the engine was bullet proof and could be cruised happily along at sixty-five without fuss. It would even hold seventy if you could bear the thought of that poor little engine thrashing away beneath you on pretty much full throttle. But since 80mph was the preferred cruising speed for most of us, I will concede that the little Honda was too slow. However, that low top speed hides a little-known and well-kept secret: its acceleration.

Away from the line, there wasn't much that could match the Benly. No, seriously; scoff if you must but up to fifteen miles per hour, the thing was a rocket. Slam open the throttle, brutally drop the clutch and it would leap away from the line like a greyhound out of the trap. Okay, 15mph isn't much, but in a crowded city street, it's all you need to get in front at the traffic light grand prix. And getting in front was all that mattered, right? Right.

Another asset was its ease of maintenance. First of all, it had a fully enclosed chain. Ugly and old fashioned-looking true, but it increased chain life by a huge margin. And when replacement time finally did come around, it was cheap – as were the long-lasting tyres. Also, I could give the engine a full service in less than half an hour, which gave me more time to spend with my kids. Drinks all round then.

The great should have been: There is one bike I want to mention, not because it was a good bike, because it was worse even than less-than-mediocre bikes like the 250 Superdream (the 400 Dreams/Superdreams were actually pretty good). It was, however, a bike that had the *potential* to be up there with the best. It *should* have been great, but was in the end a complete and utter lemon. I'm referring to the less than lamented, **Kawasaki GPZ305:**

Here was a bike that had my hand hovering over my wallet just waiting for it to get fat enough to pounce. "Wait for it, wait for it; any moment now..." The thing looked perfect; and I don't just mean aesthetically, although its sporting GPZ livery and neat bikini fairing did stir the blood. No, I'm talking specs.

The little firecracker was small and lithe. It could filter with the best and it went like the proverbial bat out of hell. It could top a ton *and* return almost seventy to the gallon. Yes, seventy! It had a pretty big tank for a small bike too. Comfort-wise it wasn't the best, but it certainly wasn't the worst. It was easy to service and had a marvellous belt final drive. All the advantages of a chain without the hassle, and none of the power-sapping weight and complexity of a shaft. Brilliant. I wanted one – no, I lusted after one. It wasn't that expensive either. Even so, I never quite had the money to buy one. Boy did I dodge a bullet there!

The problem was the engine. As great as it went, it was as fragile as a bone china teapot with a chocolate spout! A determined despatch rider could destroy one in under four thousand miles. Even in careful hands, ten thousand was an achievement. Every time you swung a leg over it you were inviting it to detonate. It seemed that just a stern look could cause a big-end failure. What on earth were Kawasaki thinking of when they let this useless piece of excrement into their showrooms? They must have known about its defects – especially as it was derived from the 1980 Z250, which was a disastrous time bomb in its own right.

So what was the cause of the problem? Quite simply it was oil circulation – or more accurately, a lack of oil circulation. This was caused by the teensy-weensy oil pickup in the sump. It just didn't allow enough of the 10w40 lifeblood to flow. Bad enough on a plodder with a lowly 8,000 rpm redline, but on an 11,000 rpm screamer? Imagine a man with a dodgy heart being forced to run a four minute mile and you'll get the idea. Adding to the circulation woes was the nylon (yes, *nylon*) cog driving the oil pump. It was just waiting for the most inopportune moment to shred its teeth. The resulting failure of just about every engine internal would be fatal beyond all resuscitation. Even our lord Jesus would struggle to resurrect it! To paraphrase Monty Python, it would be in every way an ex-bike!

You'd have thought it would be easy for Kawasaki to rectify the situation, but maybe the oil pickup problem was insurmountable, who knows. But the oil pump drive wheel? For crying out loud, how much would it have cost to replace it with a metal one? Shame on you, Kawasaki; shame on you!

But they weren't the only culprits. Suzuki produced another of the great should-have-beens in the guise of the GSX400F. Not the terrific twin that I owned, but a four cylinder lookalike. I wanted one of these simply because it combined two of my best mounts in one. My GSX400EZ, and my CB400 four.

It wasn't as delicate as the GPZ, but it too suffered from oil circulation problems. This time it was due to the sump capacity being too small. Suzuki's remedy? Would you believe it was a new oil filler cap with a shorter dipstick? So their answer was simply to overfill your engine with oil. Genius!

There were other failures on the market of course – although none quite as catastrophic as the GPZ. I cite that little Kwacker in particular (and to a lesser extent the Suzuki) because it was the one that disappointed me the most.

Others: There were far, far too many different bikes to go into detail about. You could pretty much say that if it was on the market, it was on the circuit somewhere in London. Virtually any bike would earn you some money if it was reliable enough *and* you could find a company that would employ you. I've seen everything from a Kawasaki KE100 dirt bike all the way up to a Z1300 six cylinder monster!

As time went on, and new models came onto the market, the bikes we saw the most would change as well. Except for the old Plastic Maggot, of course. That soldiered on throughout the whole decade, although the later Eurosport versions never seemed to have quite the same presence. Before I started, the Suzuki GT250 was quite popular, but there were precious few of them left by 1980. Believe it or not though, I ran a GT250A for a while in the mid-eighties.

That's really all I can think of for the moment. As I've said in a previous chapter, we bikers are a tribal lot. As such, I imagine many readers will vehemently disagree with my assertions. Or maybe I've missed out a bike that deserves a mention. In either case, my email address is on my website, spmuir.com so why not let me know. Speak to you soon.

Incidentally, Damon Hill was a dispatch rider for a while in the 80's. We rode for the same outfit and as I recall he used a red Kawasaki Z750. If you ever read this, Damon, please let me know if I've got it wrong.

12: THE WORLD'S FASTEST WRINKLY

Surreal is a word I've used quite a few times in relating my experiences. And you have to admit, some of them have been a bit Twilight Zone in appearance. Most of these odd, even supernatural (haunted MZ) events have been at best irritating, or at worst malignant. But here's one that simply puzzled and amazed.

It was a lovely summer's day; the sky was blue without a single cloud from horizon to horizon. Not that I could see the horizons, of course. As usual at that time of year, I was sitting amid the smoke and bustle of old London town, on standby, and doing nothing. It was about half-past-one and I'd only done four minimums all day. I'd have given anything for a bit of a run. Something like a Slough would have been perfect.

But wishes only come true in fairy tales, don't they?

"Three-three, three-three."

"Three-three."

"Three-three; you're on a seven-fifty, right?"

My ears pricked up. He was looking for a big bike, and there could only be one reason for that. "Yeah, roger," I said, throwing open my top box and grabbing my clipboard.

"Ready for details?"

Boy was I ready.

"Roger," I replied, hurriedly unclipping my pen. He gave me the pickup client and their Berkeley Square address, but then teasingly, he paused.

"Roger, I've got that," I said trying to gee him up to give me the destination.

"That one's going..." Again the tantalising pause. My excited anticipation was by now spinning out of control. Then eventually, with a silent but triumphant fanfare he said, "Poole in Dorset."

"Yes!" I shouted, startling the passing tourists. Then, in an effort to pay the swine back for his merciless teasing, I confirmed that I understood with an almost disdainful, "Yeah, roger."

To my delight, he sounded distinctly disappointed with my lack of reaction. "Call me pee-oh-bee," he said curtly.

Sooner than a GPZ305's engine could implode, I was on my way. And what a ride it was too; 120 miles of glory. The big (well, a 750 *was* big in its day) Suzuki simply sailed along, the subdued growl from its twin pipes gave a muted promise of the howling fun to come. I didn't hurry; why would I? I didn't want to go back to the boring, nothing to do but wait for home-time, summer lull. It was four o'clock when I eventually phoned in empty.

"Nice run?"

"Lovely."

"Off you go then; see you tomorrow."

Oh joy; could the day get any better? At that time, we were staying with my wife's mother in a village near Dartford, and I wasn't quite sure of which route to take. I pulled out my road map. "Hmm... Dorset to Kent. Let me see, how do I...?" I traced my finger along a couple of possibilities before deciding. Yes, I'd keep off the big A roads and Motorways. I'd poodle along the smaller ones and every now and then I'd give the sporty GS its head. The occasional short bit of balls-out scratching would be a great way to brighten the day even further. Gotta watch the petrol though; by my reckoning it was about a hundred and forty miles. My tank was now very low so I filled up after about ten miles of fuel-sipping, gentle-riding, limp-throttled, pottering.

"Hi-ho silver!" I shouted as I hit the road again. I hustled along at a reasonably quick pace using the Suzuki's mid-range torque to sail past any cars. The four cylinders sang a merry song as I utilised that lovely mid-range punch.

I came up behind a little sports car. I really can't tell you exactly what it was, but it looked something along the lines of a Spitfire or an MGB. I chuckled when I saw the driver flick me a look in his rear view mirror. Why were so many of these cars driven by old men? This one must be at least fifty (oh how young that sounds to me now). He had a bald head and was wearing an oddly serious expression on his silly round face. Prat!

I tucked in behind him and waited for a line of cars coming the other way to pass by. Then the road was clear; a quick flick of the wrist and I started to surge past him.

"Damn!" I snapped as the old geezer floored his accelerator. Whatever was under the bonnet of that little sports car, it had some poke! It shot away like a bullet from a gun. That was it, the gauntlet had been thrown down and I was up for the challenge.

I stamped down on the gear lever and nailed the Suzuki's throttle against the stop. The engine howled its gratitude; the rev counter rocketed towards the redline, and the speedo needle soared in sympathy. Within seconds the speed limit was left far behind in the distance. Eighty, ninety, a ton. With my chin piece rattling against the clocks I reeled the old boy in; but the faster we went, the more the advantage swung his way. By one-twenty we were accelerating at the same rate. I flattened myself even tighter against the tank but there was no way I was going get past him. *Never mind*, I thought. *As soon as we hit the twisty bits I'll have him.*

Sure enough, the long sweeping bends soon tightened bringing with them that exhilarating exercise of brake; heel it in; scrape the exhaust or stand or footrest and/or boot and then accelerate to the next bend that we bikers are so addicted to. I let loose with some most ungentlemanly expletives as the old git actually *pulled away from me!* What?!

Not to blow my own trumpet too much, but I know I was good. Not as good as my scorching-hot son, Craig, but far better than most. In my trade I had to be – all of us did. But this bald, unremarkable old geezer was blowing me away *in an effing car!*

I gritted my teeth and pushed even harder. No way was he going to beat me. Riding harder and faster than ever before, I stopped the rot and managed to stay with him. My riding was textbook. I hit every braking point and I turned in faultlessly. Everything that *could* kiss the tarmac *did* kiss the tarmac. I wound the power on at *exactly* the right moment in *exactly* the right way. Only one other time had I ridden this well (that was a hell of ride, wasn't it Paul?) but still I was unable to get in front. Who the hell was he and what was he driving?

When the road straightened out again we both let rip. We flashed past the stationary-seeming traffic at unholy speeds, but eventually, I had to concede defeat. With a reluctant sigh, I let my throttle hand go limp. "I wasn't *really* trying to pass him," I told myself unconvincingly.

Then to rub salt into the wound, as the old geezer sped away, he flashed his brake lights twice and gave me a cheery wave. With a wry smile I responded with a flash of my headlight. It had been a good game and in the end, at least I hadn't actually been beaten. Had his car actually been a fast bike, I'd have called it an honourable draw.

I settled back to my quick but unchallenging pace, eventually hitting the M25. I cut my way through the heavy motorway traffic rather too quickly and soon arrived at my mother-in-law's house. I climbed somewhat shakily from the bike. The beast's engine ticked its disappointment as it cooled down. I glanced at the cheap but accurate Casio on my wrist and did a double-take.

No way! Two hours? Really? Impossible! Impossible or not I'd covered the hundred and thirty miles from the petrol station at an average speed of sixty five mile per hour. It doesn't sound a lot, but believe me, on those roads it was incredible.

I told my friends about the encounter with the old boy but I doubt any of them believed me. I can't really blame them; I'm pretty sure I wouldn't have believed it if one of them had told the tale. But I'd been there; I'd seen him; hell, I even had the scuff-marks on my boots!

"Fancy being such a useless (expletive deleted) that you can't even beat some old fart in an MG," one of my colleagues laughed next day.

"You sure your GS ain't knackered?" another one teased.

"Must've been running on three pots," someone else chipped in.

"And beaten by an old man too."

The teasing went on mercilessly for days. I began to wish I'd never mentioned it. That old(?) boy had done more than just dent my pride, he'd crushed it! Just who the hell was he anyway?

Only one of my so-called friends eventually offered me a tiny crumb of comfort. It was a few days later and we were sitting together at my favourite spot in Irving Street. As I told him the tale he looked at me closely and nodded sagely. Then, with an enigmatic smile on his lips he said, "I reckon you just met Stirling Moss."

Whether it was the great man or not, I'll never know. But whoever you are and wherever you are; whether you're in this life or the next; sir, I salute you!

Footnote: Just as I finished writing this book, the sad news arrived that Sir Stirling Moss had passed away. I do not know if it was you I met that day, Sir Stirling, but if it was, I hope we can finish the game when I join you upstairs. Until then, my friend, may you rest in peace.

13: CREDIT WHERE CREDIT'S DUE

In spite of the financial crash, we're still living in an age of easy credit. Not quite as easy as before the melt-down of 2008, but it is still available to most. It's probably hard for anyone under twenty-five to understand just how tight it was before the restraints were lifted in 1997. The easing had begun in 1986 with the financial 'Big Bang' but it took some time to filter through to the proletariat.

Back in the day, in order to get a personal loan you first had to prove to the bank manager (remember those?) that you didn't actually need the money in the first place! Still, mortgages *were* offered and loans *were* agreed, but certainly not to us despatch rider types. It was the source of many a bitter conversation as we congregated in the stand-by haunts that littered the West End.

But in all fairness, you couldn't really blame the banks. We were paid by the parcel delivery and the available work varied drastically. On top of that, we were in one of the most dangerous occupations in the world. In one report, we were only beaten by test pilots and bomb disposal experts!

Every despatch rider needed to put a bit of money aside each week. It was necessary to cover bike maintenance, income tax, and the unpaid sickies and holidays of the self-employed worker. But the clever (single?) riders would also save up for the oft-needed new bike. However, if you were responsible for supporting a wife and kids, along with all the household bills etc. (mothers weren't expected to work in those days) things could easily go awry.

Imagine it; the work is steady and you're getting by reasonably well. With a bit of chicanery you've managed to bag a mortgage, you're earning enough to keep the wolf from the door, and you've managed to put enough aside for the necessary maintenance and the taxman. Life is as good as it gets for a D R. But then, within just a couple of weeks you're in trouble.

The problems that could raise their filthy heads were manifold, but they usually fell into three categories:

1) *Lack of work:* I've spoken about the ebb and flow of the available work, especially so in *'You're Where Now?'* but here's a recap. We humble riders were self-employed, and as I say, paid only by the package delivered. Winter was usually the busiest and most lucrative period while the summer was always quiet. But of course, even in winter you could experience a sudden and unexplainable downturn in business.

2) *Mechanical breakdowns:* With the miles we used to cover, a mechanical breakdown was pretty much inevitable at some point in the year. One could only hope it wasn't going to be a major one. As it happens, you could often plan ahead because a lot of models had recurring faults. Some were known to the manufacturers and/or motorcycle press, while others only seemed to happen to us despatchers. Certain models' problems were another subject that was often discussed by us all ad nauseam.

3) *Health.* Ah yes, health. As you can imagine, getting cold and wet day after day can really take

a toll on the old immune system. A common cold can quickly develop into something far more serious. One winter I developed a heavy cold and boy, did I feel rough. It didn't help that it was close to freezing all day and it kept trying to snow. My throat got so painful that I even had trouble swallowing water.

"I think I'm going to have to stay at home for a couple of days," I told the wife. She was less than amused, I can tell you.

"Don't think you're going to sit around here all day," she snapped. "We've got bills to pay, and you've just spent a fortune on that bloody bike!"

That last part was true; I had just spent a tidy sum. I'd bought a new tyre, as well as a chain and sprockets. *And* I'd had the temerity to give my nice blue Suzuki GS400 (yes Gary, it *was* a 400) a much needed service. On the face of it, her reaction does sound extremely harsh, but as she so rightly said, we had bills to pay.

And so it was that with a hacking cough, a croaking voice, and my nose dripping all over my Rukka jacket, I carried on. And so it was that after just one more day of freezing my bits off, I ended up in hospital for a week. That was followed by a week in bed at home, and then another few days convalescing. To her credit, she was almost apologetic... almost.

But I digress. Back to the point of this little section. As I say, there you are, merrily plodding along happily (or as happily as you can plod along in a freezing winter) and then the work dries up. The wage packet shrinks accordingly, and it doesn't matter how much your better half demands that, "You'll just have to work harder." If the bookings aren't there, the bookings aren't there! Then wham bam, thank you ma'am, the bike goes bang. Not an annoying puncture, not an expensive but manageable new part; no, we're talking full on, terminal engine disintegration. Perhaps your gearbox has exploded or your cam-chain has snapped destroying your cylinder head and worse. Then, my friend, you are well and truly up Effluence Creek without a propulsion implement.

Nowadays, I guess you'd just pop to the second hand bike shop and put a half decent hack on your credit card. Back then though, it wasn't that simple. You could crawl to your bank manager on your hands and knees and beg for his help, but I have to say this never worked for me. In fact, to be honest, I only ever knew one person that it *did* work for. And he almost died from shock when the man with the money said "yes."

So unless you worked for one the very rare companies that would lend you a few hundred quid to buy a cheap bike, your options were pretty limited. You could rent one, which was okay in the busy periods but far too expensive when it was slack. And renting was only ever a stop-gap solution anyway. You could plead with your parents to help you out if they could; or if you were very, very lucky, a good friend would sometimes help you out.

"All very interesting," I hear you say. "But what exactly is the point of this chapter?" Well it's nothing more than this. I may not have been able to *get* credit back then, but I can certainly *give* credit where it's due now.

Several times during my despatch riding years the brown and smelly well and truly hit my life's particular fan; and when it did, I was extremely fortunate. My heroic dad was good enough to bail me out more than once, so thank you dad. And I did have a couple of very, very good friends. Gary and Paul, you will always have my immense and undying gratitude; thanks lads.

14: HAPPY DAYS

Within the two collections of anecdotes I've written so far, you might get the impression that it was all doom and gloom. *'You're Where Now?'* could be particularly morose at times. Yes it's true, some of the worst and more horrific events have left deep scars – some of them physical; but there were good times. Let's face it, if there weren't, I doubt any of us would have lasted.

I can remember winter days when it was dry and not too cold. The work would be coming in at an exhilarating yet not overwhelming rate. Your own personal cash register would go 'kerching' with every letter or parcel delivered, and your good old bike would keep thrumming away reliably between your legs. Best of all, 'er indoors would be happy too. You'd arrive home incredibly tired and dirty, but at the same time immensely satisfied.

Even when it was slack in the summer, there were good times. As long as you were able to keep your head above water, the better weather would make up for the lack of money. Those particular summer days were the times when you remembered the *true* love in your life. Your bike was no longer just a means to pecuniary ends, it was once again your lover. The thrill of the romance returned. You stroked her when you cleaned her; you wooed her when you serviced her; and when you got her out on a run...

Whoops, I was getting a bit carried away there; but you get the idea anyway.

I can recall one day in particular. The sun was shining and my old Honda 400 Dream was running as sweet as a pot of honey in a candy store. It was indeed living up to its epithet. My jacket was open and my hands were bare as I wended my way happily through the Hertfordshire countryside. It was the second day that my favourite controller had given me a bit of a run. I wouldn't say I was being 'fed' as such, but he was certainly keeping me happy.

It was one of those rare times when your riding really comes together. You ride the torque, not the redline; every gear change is slick and timed to perfection; the line through every bend is just right; not a single braking point can be bettered. You all know what I'm talking about.

"God I love this job," someone said, making me jump. It took a second or two to realise that it was me. Oh yes, happy days *could* be found. Why can't it be those ones that now fill my dreams?

Printed in Great Britain
by Amazon